THEMES
for early years

GROWING

JENNY MORRIS

THEMES
for early years

Author Jenny Morris

Editors Noel Pritchard and Joel Lane

Assistant editor Libby Weaver

Series designer Lynne Joesbury

Designer Sue Stockbridge

Cover illustration Lynne Joesbury

Illustrations Sue Woollatt

Designed using Aldus Pagemaker

Processed by Scholastic Limited, Leamington Spa

Printed in Great Britain by The Alden Press, Oxford

Thanks to Barbara Dick and Jim Morris, who have given me invaluable help with Growing

Published by Scholastic Limited, Villiers House, Clarendon Avenue, Leamington Spa, Warwickshire CV32 5PR

© 1996 Scholastic Ltd.   Text © 1996 Jenny Morris

2 3 4 5 6 7 8 9   6 7 8 9 0

The publishers gratefully acknowledge permission to reproduce the following copyright material:
© 1996 **Clive Barnwell** for 'Clomp! Stomp! Tromperty Tromp!', 'Dingle, dangle scarecrow' and 'Count the rings'; © 1996 **Debbie Campbell** for 'Grandad loves his garden'; © 1996 **John Foster** for 'The bean seed' and 'The balloon', included by permission of the author; © 1996 **Lesley Funge** for 'A brand new baby'; © 1996 **Jean Gilbert** for 'Caterpillar' and 'Tadpole'; © 1996 **Gillian Goddard** for 'Grow up!'; © 1996 **Carole Henderson-Begg** for 'A seed'; © 1995 **Jan Holdstock** for 'The three little pigs', 'Dandelion clock' and 'Growing up'; © 1994 **Jan Jones** for 'Petra's room' and 'When I was a baby'; © 1996 **Karen King** for 'Growing flowers'; **Kingfisher** for 'The enormous turnip' by Susan Price from *Kingfisher Treasury of Nursery Stories* edited by Susan Price © Susan Price (1994, Kingfisher); © 1994 **Fiona McGarry** for 'Daisy chain' and 'Garden rainbow', originally published in *Child Education* (May 1994, Scholastic Ltd.); © 1995 **Tony Mitton** for 'The crop song', 'One day (when I grow up)', 'The farmer knows' and 'Grown out of'; © 1995 **Judith Nicholls** for 'A seedy story' and 'The planter'; © 1993 **Sue Nicholls** words and music for 'The sunflower song' and © 1995 Sue Nicholls words for 'Savings grow!' © 1996 **Jan Pollard** for 'Birthdays'; © 1996 **Lesley Prior** for collective worship ideas, three approaches; © 1996 **Ruth Silvestre** for 'Alexander's growing up day'.
Every effort has been made to trace copyright holders and the publishers apologise for any inadvertent omissions.

British Library Cataloguing-in-Publication Data A catalogue record for this book is available from the British Library.
ISBN 0-590-53384-3

CONTENTS

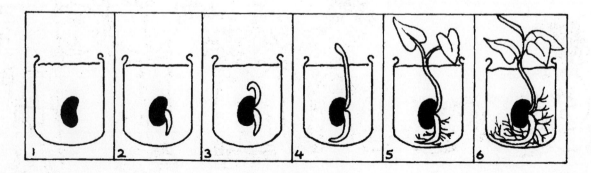

INTRODUCTION

GROWING

'Where do peas come from?' Try asking this question of the children in your group and see how often their answer will be 'A tin' or 'Out of the freezer'. If your next question is 'Where do they come from before they are put in the tin or freezer?' you are likely to be told that peas are made in a factory.

In this book, children can discover that peas are vegetables which grow in pods and that all vegetables are plants which grow in the ground. Children's natural curiosity promotes learning and what can be more intriguing than waiting for a seed to sprout, seeing newly-hatched chicks peck for food or watching frog spawn turn from 'full stops' into 'commas' and then into tadpoles? A topic on 'Growing' introduces many surprises which will enable children to appreciate the magic of creation.

Many of the activities in this book use natural materials which the children can look out for as they walk to playgroup, school or shops. This will encourage them to notice the minute daily changes of nature and to discover the natural life cycles which surround them. Perhaps this theme will foster a lifetime's joy and interest in natural history.

AIMS

This book provides activities for young children who are either in nurseries, playgroups, at home, or in school reception classes. It aims to help introduce concepts about growing in a practical way which will stimulate children and adults supervising the activities. If the adults are enthusiastic, the children in their care will be eager to make their own discoveries, to use their senses and find out about the miracles of nature. Each chapter in the book presents different aspects of the theme of growing.

Chapter One: I'm Growing Up concentrates on growth in human beings, their wants, needs and capabilities. It starts from birth and covers the stages of learning to walk, talk and play with others, which the children will know about. It gives the children a chance to talk and think about their futures as adults and as old people. Chapter Two covers the life cycles (metamorphoses) of butterflies and frogs. It looks at the development of other young animals and includes their feeding habits, movement, and dependency (or otherwise) on their parents. The children will be able to make comparisons between the different types of animals and to look for similarities between animals growing and themselves. In Chapter Three, seeds and plants are investigated by carrying out simple scientific experiments. The children will be able to examine the parts of plants and discover how much patience is necessary when you want to grow them. Chapter Four looks at how the growth of trees and flowers is dependent on the seasons and the condition of the soil in which they grow. The children will hear about the variety of creatures which are an important part of tree life. They will be given garden tools and shown how to use them safely, and will also be encouraged to make their own mini-garden. Chapter Five takes a look at farming and how basic foods such as cereals, fruit and vegetables are produced. A supermarket game gives the children a chance to look at foods which have been grown abroad and varieties of food that are eaten by other ethnic groups. Chapter Six shows children that many of the things they use every day, such as paper, wool and cotton, come from growing plants, as do other things such as cork and herbs.

HOW TO USE THIS BOOK

This book about Growing is one title in a series of *Themes for Early Years* books. It is presented as a 'package deal' because it contains everything that is needed for a topic on this theme: activity ideas and photocopiable sheets, poems, stories, songs, and practical suggestions for assemblies and displays. This means that you do not need to search round frantically for suitable books in order to use this theme with children.

There are eight main activities in each of the first six chapters. Most of the activity pages are independent of the other pages (except the butterfly and frog life cycles) therefore they do not have to be used in sequential order.

All groups are different and for some it may be suitable to complete one Growing activity every day for several weeks. Others may prefer to dip into the book now and again according to mood and to the season. Either way, let the book work for you and fit in with your style.

TOPIC WEB

The topic web on pages 8–9 categorises the activities in this book according to their main focus which may be Maths, English, Science, Technology, Music, Art, PE, RE, Geography and History. Although each activity page has a main focus many of the ideas are cross-curricular. This topic web can be photocopied and used as a guide and check-list of what you have completed and what is still to be covered. It will help with planning towards the National Curriculum and Scottish 5–14 Guidelines.

ACTIVITY PAGES

All of the activities in the first six chapters follow a standard format and include sections on Objective, Group size, What you need, What to do, Discussion and Follow-up activities.

The Objectives specify in which area of the curriculum the activity concentrates and also describes what the activity will teach.

Young children have a limited attention span and need to be actively involved in a project to maintain their concentration. With this in mind small group sizes have been recommended except where an activity can involve everyone. These recommendations are only guidelines, and need not be followed rigidly, you will know best how your children function.

It will be a great help if you plan well ahead to see 'what you need' and start collecting resources early to ensure out of season availability! Wherever possible re-cyclable or garden materials are used, and where this is not possible, costs have been kept to a minimum. Tell the children in advance what you will be doing and the anticipation will generate a lot of excitement and pleasure. Ask them to collect and bring in the items that are needed (where appropriate). This will give them a sense of responsibility, and at the same time involve their parents.

Occasionally, activities require advance preparation. This has been kept to a minimum and it may be that the children themselves can do it.

Try to let the children do as much as possible, and is safe for them, in the 'What to do' sections. When plants and seeds are used in an activity quick-growing varieties have been suggested. The span of time is a very difficult concept for a young child to comprehend and waiting for something to grow can seem endless!

The 'Discussion' sections can be used as a starting-point for language development with the children. Give them time to contribute their own ideas and anecdotes about growing.

Follow-up activities are sometimes used to extend and reinforce the main activity at the time, but often extra ideas are given which can be completed at a later date.

DISPLAYS

Young children are very self-centred and love to be able to take home their work and show what they have been doing. Sometimes, however, there is a valuable social aspect in sharing their work with other children. The ideas suggested in the 'Displays' chapter concentrate on aspects of growing which are suitable for a group project. There are also general hints on planning, mounting and enhancing a display.

ASSEMBLIES

In the same way that display activities concentrate on producing group work, assemblies are another way of learning to share experiences. The ideas in this chapter will enable children to perform collectively on the theme of 'Growing'. Working together is an important aspect of growing up.

THE RESOURCES SECTION

Action rhymes, poems, stories and songs about 'Growing' are provided in this section. They may be photocopied and used with the activities where suggested or may be used at any other time independently.

PHOTOCOPIABLE ACTIVITY SHEETS

There are eight pages of games and activities which can be photocopied for use with specific activities within the theme. Some of the games can be re-used and will benefit from being copied on to card and covered with adhesive plastic film. Many of the activities on these pages can be adapted or used in ways other than those suggested.

RECOMMENDED MATERIALS

This page lists the titles of information books, stories, poems, music and songs which are relevant but not essential to the theme of 'Growing'. They could be very useful as additional resource material.

EXPRESSIVE ARTS

Planning towards the National Curriculum and the Scottish National Guidelines 5-14

PREPARING FOR PRIMARY SCHOOL

THE NATIONAL CURRICULUM

When children enter compulsory state schooling at the age of five, they will start work on the National Curriculum. It is intended that any child will be able to go to school anywhere in the country and find the same areas of the curriculum being covered for the same amount of time each week.

The subjects of the National Curriculum are: English, Mathematics, Science, History, Geography, Design and technology, Information technology, RE, Art, Music and PE. There is a Programme of Study (guidance on what should be taught) for each subject, and teachers assess the level of attainment of each child when they reach Year Two (age six to seven). This is done partly through nationwide tests, but mostly by asking teachers to use their judgement to allocate an overall level to each child.

The activities in this book have been specially written to give a firm foundation for the early stages of the National Curriculum. Whether the children are looking at plants or making a simple boat out of cork, they will be gaining an excellent preparation for later learning at school.

It is important not to overlook the value of learning through the medium of play. All the activities in this book aim to engage the children in exciting and enjoyable new learning experiences.

Each activity has a clear learning objective which is linked to the relevant National Curriculum subject area. You will find the division into subject areas on the topic web on pages 8 and 9.

THE SCOTTISH 5–14 NATIONAL GUIDELINES

In Scotland, there are National Guidelines for schools on what should be taught to children between the ages of five and fourteen.

These National Guidelines are divided into six main curriculum areas: English language, Mathematics, Environmental studies, Expressive arts, Religious and moral education, Personal and social development.

Within these main areas further subjects are to be found; for example, 'Expressive arts' includes art and design, drama, music and PE. Strands are also identified within each subject; for example, 'Mathematics' includes 'problem-solving and enquiry' and 'shape, position and movement'.

Most nurseries and playgroups will find that the experiences they are offering children will lay a good foundation for this curriculum. This book provides activities which have been specially written to prepare for the many aspects of the curriculum, and which will also fit well into the pre-five curriculum guidelines issued by many local authorities throughout Scotland.

To help you with your planning, the individual activities have been allocated to separate areas of the curriculum shown in the Topic Web on pages 8 and 9. The children's personal and social development is an ongoing theme that is incorporated throughout the book.

CHAPTER 1
I'M GROWING UP

Children already have plenty of evidence that they are growing. They need their hair and nails cutting when they have grown too long. They need bigger clothes when they have grown out of the ones they are wearing. This chapter covers the stages of human growth from birth through childhood to adults and into old age.

CLEAN NAPPIES

Objective

Mathematics – To make a picture of nappies hanging on a washing line and to introduce the children to subtraction.

Group size

Ten children.

What you need

Pieces of card, some nylon string, a pair of scissors, a stapler, glue, an old towelling nappy or white towel, pencils.

Preparation

Cut a piece of A4-size card lengthways to make it approximately 10cm × 29cm. Cut a piece of string 35cm in length and tie a single knot at each end. Staple the string to each end of the card strip to make a 'washing line'. One washing line will be needed for each child. Cut the nappy up into 4cm squares, allowing five squares for each child.

What to do

Sing this rhyme with the children to the tune of 'Five Currant Buns in a Baker's Shop'.

> *Five dirty nappies in the washing machine,*
> *Spinning around until they are clean,*
> *Hang them on the line, it's a lovely day,*
> *Along comes the wind and blows one away.*

(Count down to 'no dirty nappies', then sing)
> *No dirty nappies in the washing machine,*
> *Spinning around until they are clean.*
> *None for the line on this lovely day,*
> *None for the wind to blow right away.*

Let the children count out five nappy squares and stick them on to their card as if they were hanging them on the line. They can write the numbers one to five underneath the nappies and draw little 'roof tops' for the pegs as shown in the diagram. Practise subtraction with the children by covering up each nappy after it has blown away. They could count down on their fingers to reinforce this. Show them how to clench their fist to represent nothing and how this is written as a zero in maths language.

Discussion

Talk about what new babies are like. Why do they need nappies? Can the children think of other things that new babies are able to do: blink, open and close their eyes, see, breathe, sneeze, smell, wrinkle their nose, suck, burp, taste, yawn, dribble, hear, feel hot or cold, feel pain, grip a finger. Do the children know what babies need to grow (remember love)? What things are babies able to do as they grow older? Ask different children to describe events in a baby's routine, such as bathtime.

Follow-up activities

Encourage the children to:
✧ Crawl and roll over like a baby.
✧ Make a mobile for a baby. Brush glue on to a fir cone, add glitter and hang it from the ceiling.
✧ Make up a name starting with each letter of the alphabet for an imaginary baby.
✧ Make a clothes line between two chairs. The children can 'peg out' the dressing-up clothes.
✧ Sing the song 'A brand new baby' in the Resources section on page 81.

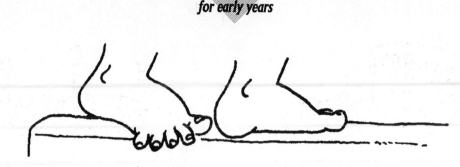

BALANCING ACT

Objective

Physical Education — To practise balancing in different ways.

Group size

Ten children.

What you need

A long school bench or a strong plank and four clean house bricks.

What to do

Place one brick under each end of the plank. Ask the children to take it in turns to walk along it. At first they may keep their arms at their sides — suggest that they stretch them out at either side to help balance themselves. For those who have very good balance, let them try walking across a higher plank which is resting on two bricks at each end. Then remove the bricks from under one end and let the children try walking up or down the sloping plank. Show them how to balance in other ways (not on the plank) stand on one leg then stand on the other leg; crouch down with bent knees and try 'walking' in this position (keeping hands off the floor); kneel on the floor lifting your feet off the ground behind you; sit on the floor with arms folded and legs outstretched in front but raised slightly off the ground.

Discussion

Ask the children which way they found easiest to walk along the plank. Did their outstretched arms help them to balance? Can anyone describe what happens when a baby tries to walk (wobbles, stumbles)? The children were toddlers once themselves and had to learn how to balance. Why is it easy for them to walk now? Do they know why a newly-born foal needs to find its balance very quickly? When a young bird is ready to leave the nest it takes little practice flights to learn how to balance when flying. Can they think of any people who are especially good at balancing (ballet dancers, gymnasts, ice skaters, skiers, footballers, horse riders)? Why do some older people use a walking stick? Have any of the children ever tried balancing on anything else (for example: a fallen tree trunk)?

Follow-up activities

✧ Cut up a copy of photocopiable page 89 for each child and ask them to arrange the pictures in age sequence.
✧ Ask the children to cross arms, hold hands and spin round and round with a partner. Can they stand still afterwards or do they feel too dizzy?
✧ Tell the children to choose a friend to play with on the see-saw. Can they balance it in mid-air?
✧ Sing and play the 'Hokey Cokey' from *Oranges and Lemons* compiled by Karen King (OUP).
✧ Try walking backwards — be careful!
✧ Read the poem 'When I was a baby' on page 70 of the Resources section.

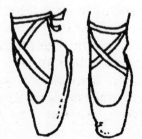

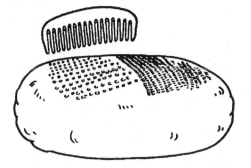

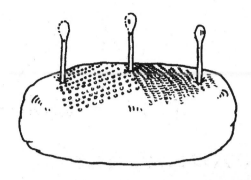

HAPPY BIRTHDAY TO YOU

Objective

Mathematics – To make a clay birthday cake with 'candles' which will help the children to understand that as numbers get bigger they increase in value.

Group size

Six children.

What you need

Clay, a laminated or wooden board, a jug of water, a comb, a pointed tool or pencil, cotton buds, a pair of scissors, paint and brushes, PVA glue to use as a glaze.

Preparation

Prepare a piece of clay approximately the same size as a golf ball for each child. Cut the cotton buds in half to serve as 'candles' for the birthday cakes. (Each child will need sufficient candles to represent their age.)

What to do

Let the children enjoy playing with the clay by pulling, pinching and rolling it. If it starts to get too dry, wet it slightly with fingertips dipped in water. Tell them to roll it into a ball and then squash it flat with the palm of their hand. Use the comb or a pointed tool to mark indentations in the clay 'cake' for decoration.

Each child should count out the same number of cotton bud candles as their age and then stick them into the cake. Initial each child's cake on the base.

Leave the clay to dry for 24 hours. When the cakes are dry, let the children choose which colour they want to paint them. When the paint is thoroughly dry (not long because the clay is very absorbent) brush on a glaze of watered-down PVA glue. (Don't worry if it looks white, it will be clear when it dries.)

Sing 'Happy Birthday' to whoever is having a pretend birthday! Clap your hands and count for each candle that there is on the cake.

Discussion

Ask the children why we celebrate birthdays. Do they know when their birthday is and how old they will be on their next birthday? How old were they last year? Each year they have one more candle on their birthday cake to show that they are growing older. In what other ways can they tell they are growing older? Remind the children that they must never touch or play with matches or lighters because they could be badly hurt. Emphasise that the candles they have stuck in their clay cake are pretend and not made of wax. Nobody should ever try to light them.

Follow-up activities

✧ Have a pretend birthday party in the home corner.
✧ Play 'pass the parcel' with a surprise present hidden in the wrapping.
✧ Use a candle to make a wax resist picture.
✧ Cut a real cake into pieces showing how to make halves, quarters and eighths.
✧ Wrap up some presents and ask the children to try to guess what's in them from their shape.
✧ Read the poem 'Birthdays' on page 71 of the Resources section, and the poem 'Growing Up' in *When We Were Very Young* by A. A. Milne (Methuen).

A GROWING ALPHABET

Objective

English – To compile an alphabet of the things children need to grow, to help initial sound recognition.

Group size

Twelve children.

What you need

The poem 'What Are Little Boys Made Of, What Are Little Girls Make Of' (*The Oxford Nursery Rhyme Book* assembled by Iona and Peter Opie). A board to display the lower-case alphabet letters, either written or pinned up.

What to do

Read the poem aloud to the children. Establish that the ideas in the poem are only for fun, and explain that you are going to make up an alphabet with them of what is really needed for children to grow up healthy. Ask them which letter comes first in the alphabet and then write 'a' on the board. Can they think of something beginning with 'a' that they need to have, or be allowed to do, to help them to grow up? Repeat this process for the whole of the alphabet. One possible alphabetic list of needs is shown on the right.

Discussion

Obviously, it must be pointed out to the children that some of the suggested items may only be needed occasionally! Talk through the list and ask the children why each of these things is necessary. What would happen if they didn't have some of these things? Safety is an important need – how do the children think they should behave to ensure their own safety? Many of the suggestions may be to do with feelings and perhaps the children can give examples of when they have felt like this. It can be invaluable for young children to talk through their feelings, especially the negative ones, and see that they are still acceptable members of the group. Discuss the extra needs of disabled people: ramps for wheelchairs, textured paving stones for the blind at road crossings, hearing aids for the deaf, inhalers for people with asthma.

(show) **a**nger
breathe
cry
drink
explore
(eat) **f**ood
give
(a) **h**ouse
injections
jolly
kiss
love
milk
(be) **n**aughty
(to) **o**wn
play
(be) **q**uiet
rest
sun
talk
(be) **u**ntidy
vegetables
wish
e**x**ercise
yawn
zest (enjoyment and excitement)

Follow-up activities

✧ Make a class alphabet book of 'needs', illustrated by the children.
✧ Stretch their imagination. Each child can pick a different creature and make up phrases such as:
If I were a snail I'd need to be strong enough to carry a house on my back.
If I were a spider I'd need lots of pairs of shoes.
If I were a giraffe I'd need to have my food kept high.
If I were a frog I'd need to be able to swim.
✧ Children can act out some of the feelings, or the teacher can act out feelings and then ask the children what s/he's doing.
✧ Read the story 'Petra's room' and the poem 'Grown out of' in the Resources section on pages 80 and 72.
✧ Sing 'At half past three we go home to tea' from *Someone's Singing, Lord* (A & C Black).

BODY-BUILDING

∗ ∗

Objective

Mathematics — To recognise numbers 1 to 6 and match them to the picture of a body outline as part of a game.

Group size

Six children.

What you need

One body outline from photocopiable sheet 90 for each child, pencils, a dice numbered 1 to 6 and a shaker.

What to do

Give each child a copy of the body outline and a pencil. Ask them to point to each number (on their sheet) as you call it out. Then go through the body parts (on the sheet) and ask them to point to these. Explain to them that they are going to take turns to throw the dice and that when they do so they should call out the number they have thrown and then draw over the dotted lines of the body shape which matches the number on the dice. They should only draw round one shape at a time, therefore they must throw numbers 3, 4 and 5 twice. If they throw a number that has already been used up they either have to wait until their next turn or they can continue throwing the dice until they get a number they haven't yet thrown. The rules depend on the age and patience of the children. When they have outlined the whole body they can fill in the features of the face.

Discussion

Ask the children whether they would have been able to play this game when they were babies. Why not? Talk about the skills that they have used in playing this game. They have recognised numbers, held a pencil and drawn with it, used the dice and shaker. What other things have they learned since they became old enough to go to school / nursery / playgroup? Discuss what our bodies are made of and the function of bones. Talk about disability — not all children have two arms and two legs. How do they manage?

Follow-up activities

✧ Using photocopiable sheet on page 90, blank out the numbers and substitute them for letters: H for head, C for cap, F for feet, and so on. Alter the dice correspondingly and play a letter version of this game.

✧ Play a body-building game that involves drawing each part (i.e., without the pre-drawn outline). Players need to throw a 1 at first to draw the main body before moving on to the other parts.

✧ Each child can make their own jigsaw from the body outline. Colour it, cut it into pieces, re-assemble it and then if the children wish they can stick it back together on to a piece of coloured paper.

✧ Tell the story of 'The Gingerbread Man', and then hold a cookery session to bake some gingerbread men.

✧ Read the story *Funnybones* by Janet and Allan Ahlberg (Mammoth).

✧ Sing the action song 'Growing up' on page 85 of the Resources section.

FOR MY FRIEND

Objective

Religious Education – To make a folded paper gift for a friend and discover the joy of giving.

Group size

Six children.

What you need

A 21cm square of white paper, pencils, fibre-tipped pens, pastel and wax crayons.

What to do

Fold the paper square in half diagonally and then in half again. Open it out and you can see the middle of the square where the folds meet. Fold each corner into this middle point and press down the edges (see Figure 1). Now fold the new corners into the middle of this smaller square, pressing the edges hard each time (see Figure 2). Decorate the four triangles, holding them down to stop them 'springing up'. Try to make each triangle look the same with a line or circle going through all the triangles (see Figure 3). Open out these triangles and decorate the layer underneath in similar fashion. Open out this second layer of triangles and write 'from –––––' (child's name) in the middle of the square. Fold all the triangles up again, turn the present over and write the name of the friend receiving the present on the outside. Give the folded surprise to your friend.

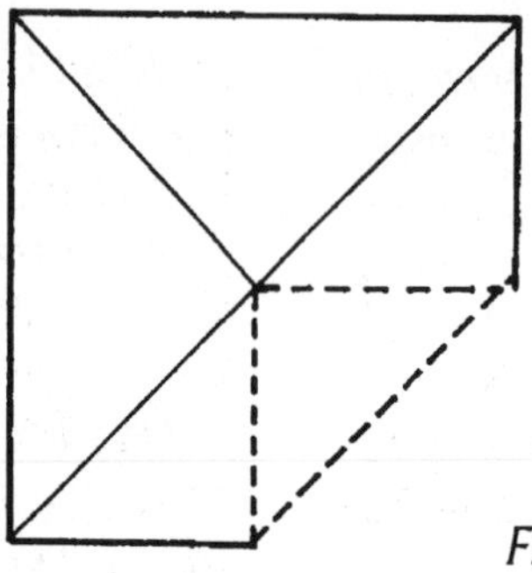

Figure 1

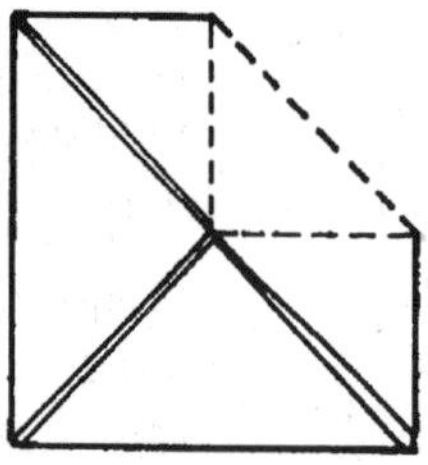

Figure 2

Figure 3

Discussion

Have all the children managed to give away the gift they have made? It can be very hard for a young child to give something away that they have just spent time in making. Ask them who gives things to them – parents, grandparents, siblings? Try to help them to understand that giving does not always concern material things. The most valuable thing that we can give to each other is our time, like the time that they have just spent in making a surprise for their friend. If their friend was pleased with the gift, how did he or she show it? Sometimes friends swap things. This means that they give each other something precious of their own. Often they swap them back again after a few days. Discuss the importance of friendship. Do the children ever quarrel with their friend and, if so, what about? How do they 'make up' again? Talk about the special times for giving at birthdays and festivals.

Follow-up activities

✧ Play some board games like Snakes and Ladders or Ludo.
✧ Let the children play a game of 'tag' 'outside with friends.
✧ Tell the children to play 'Follow My Leader' behind you – going slowly, quickly, hopping, skipping and jumping.
✧ Ask the children to take ten construction blocks and share them out between them. How many will each have?
✧ Two friends can play on a see-saw and sing 'See-saw Marjorie Daw'.
✧ If the children could give someone a lovely present, what would it be and who would they give it to?
✧ Read the story 'Alexander's Growing-up Day' on page 75 of the Resources section.
✧ Read the poem 'The morning walk' in *Now We Are Six* by A. A. Milne (Methuen).

WHEN I'M GROWN-UP

* *

Objective

Drama – To play fantasy games with the dressing-up clothes and to encourage the children to think about the future.

Group size

Twelve children.

What you need

Some dressing-up clothes which might include some of the following: lace, ribbons, a cloak, gloves, socks, stockings, tights, belts, hats, helmets, grown-up shoes, scarves, shirts, shawls, net curtains. Collect together some 'props' such as: an umbrella, a walking stick, a handbag, jewellery, spectacles (without lenses), goggles, a toy toolbox, a toy stethoscope, a shoe measure, a small suitcase, hair rollers, a full-length mirror if possible.

What to do

Allow the children to go through the range of clothes and props. Ask them to choose the clothes that they might wear when they are grown-up and have a job. Give the children a free rein when choosing their outfits, even if they look nothing like a person doing the job. When they have all chosen something to wear, and have been helped into their outfits, call the group together. Pick a confident child first and ask the others to guess what she is dressed up as. Sing the following song to the tune of 'Lavender's Blue', and allow each child in turn to sing the part of their 'character'.

> When I grow up dilly dilly,
> I'm going to be,
> A doctor in white (a plumber who mends,
> a pop star who sings, and so on) dilly dilly.
> You wait and see.

Let the children keep their dressing-up clothes on for the rest of the morning while they carry out their normal routine. Encourage them to put the clothes away carefully at the end.

Discussion

Talk about what the children's parents and grandparents do either at home or out at work. Do the children know what people actually do when they work in an office, a hospital, an orchestra or other positions? Why do people work? Discuss jobs that require special clothes or uniforms and why these might be needed. Are the children aware that some jobs are dangerous? Talk through the hazards of collecting rubbish, mending roads, re-wiring houses, handling money. To avoid alarm, explain that safety measures are taken.

Dressing up is a good opportunity to explore the make-believe world that children have been hearing about in fairy stories.

Follow-up activities

✧ Play a game of job association – hold up different equipment such as a spanner, a hair roller, a rolling pin, a garden trowel, a calculator and a body thermometer, and ask 'Who uses this?'
✧ Help the children to act out a little story in their dressing-up clothes.
✧ Read the poem 'One day when I grow up' on page 73 of the Resources section.

SING A SONG OF SIXPENCE

● ●

Objective

History – To make coin impressions and learn about how money (in one currency) has changed since the children's grandparents were young.

Group size

Six children.

What you need

Coins from the past (these are often available from flea markets or antique sales), such as an old penny, a ha'penny, a farthing, a threepenny bit, a sixpence and a shilling, coins which are in present-day use, some Plasticine or Blu-Tack, aluminium foil, thick and thin pencils, wax crayons, candle stubs.

Preparation

Cut a piece of foil about 15cm by 20cm for each child (allow one or two extra pieces).

What to do

Squash a tiny ball of Blu-Tack on to a table top or flat surface. Press a coin on to it and place a piece of foil over the coin. Stretch the foil with the finger and thumb of one hand on each side of the coin. Use the thin pencil to scratch gently backwards and forwards on the foil covering the coin. You will see an impression of the coin appearing on the foil. It will be clearer if the children move their pencil in one direction only, however they can run the point of the pencil around the inside of the rim to give a good outline. Experiment making impressions with several different coins, both old and new, using the thick pencil, crayon, candle and your fingernail.

Discussion

Allow the children to handle and examine the old coins to look at the different kings' and queens' heads. See if they can read the year in which the coins were minted (made). Money has changed since their grandparents were young. Compare the sizes, the metal colours and weights of the old coins with those in current use. What else has changed since their grandparents were young? (Colour television, telephone dials, video recorders, calculators, computers, car alarms, clothes, toys.) How can you tell if people and things are old? Who is the oldest person they know, and who is the youngest?

Follow-up activities

✧ Keep your eyes shut while you pick a coin from a bag. Feel the edge and its size. Can you tell what coin it is?

✧ Ask a child to tell the class about a 'memory' that their grandparents have told them.

✧ Look at an old photo to see the way fashion, clothes and hairstyles have changed.

✧ Sing 'Pop Goes the Weasel' and 'Sing a Song of Sixpence'.

✧ Draw a penny-farthing bike.

✧ Bring some coins from other currencies into school. Find the countries these currencies belong to on the map.

✧ Read the story 'Grow up!' on page 78 of the Resources section.

✧ Sing the song 'Savings grow!' on page 82 of the Resources section.

Teachers' note: decimal currency was introduced in 1971. Comparative values are as follows:

4 farthings = 2 ha'pennies = 1 old penny.

12 old pennies = 1 shilling = 5p.

20 shillings = 1 pound = 100p.

CHAPTER 2
GROWTH IN ANIMALS

Most mammals can easily be recognised in their adult form which is similar to how they were as babies. However some creatures such as the butterfly and the moth change completely during their growing lives. This chapter on animal growth will enable the children to look for similarities and differences between their growing up and that of animals.

WHO'S MY MOTHER?

Objective

English – To play an animal sounds game which will enable children to match baby animals to their parents.

Group size

Five children.

What you need

The story *Are You My Mother?* by P. D. Eastman (Harper Collins, 1993). A copy of photocopiable sheet on page 91, a piece of card on which to mount the sheet, adhesive plastic film (optional), a pair of scissors.

Preparation

Stick the photocopied sheet on to the card and cover it with the adhesive plastic film. Cut the card along the dotted lines so that you have a pack of eight cards with an animal on each one.

What to do

Gather the children round and read them the story *Are You my Mother?* This is the story of a baby bird that falls from its nest and approaches many different creatures in search of its mother. Be sure that the children know the sounds that a pig, duck, sheep and cow make.

Sort the animal cards into 'parents' and 'offspring' sets. Give four of the children a parent card each and tell them not to show it to the others. Let the fifth child choose one of the offspring cards and look at it but keep it hidden from the others. This child now goes to one of the 'parents' who will make the sound of the animal on their card, if it matches his offspring card he will repeat the noise to show he has found his parent. If the parent sound doesn't match his animal he should move on to the next 'parent' until he finds the sound that matches. The newly-found parent can exchange his card for an offspring card, and the four other children change their parent cards. Each time an offspring finds a parent, the parent becomes the new offspring.

Discussion

The baby animals in the game found their parents by making the same noises. Can the children think of any other ways in which parents and offspring can recognise each other? Young animals often look just like their parents, but not always. Does a young chick look like a mother hen, a cygnet like a swan, a tadpole like a frog, a caterpillar like a butterfly, or a newborn kangaroo like its mother? Sniffing is very important to some young animals who can recognise their mothers by smell.

Follow-up activities

✧ Give each child a copy of photocopiable page 91 and let them draw lines to match the animal parent with its young. They can then colour them.
✧ Tell the story of 'The Ugly Duckling'.
✧ Introduce collective terms: a flock of sheep, a herd of cows, a gaggle of geese, a litter of puppies.

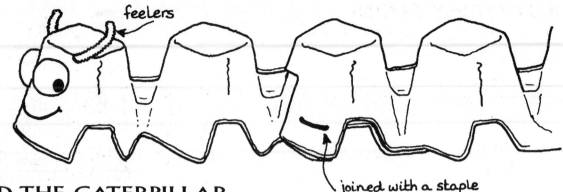

feelers

joined with a staple

FIND THE CATERPILLAR

Objective

Design and Technology — To make an egg-carton caterpillar and paint it in a colour chosen to blend with a background for camouflage.

Group size

Eight children.

What you need

Pictures of caterpillars or a real one (see * below). Plenty of large egg-carton trays, scissors, a stapler, a metal skewer, half a pipe-cleaner for each child, PVA glue, buttons or pieces of felt for eyes, different-coloured powder paints mixed thickly, brushes.

Discussion

Have any of the children ever seen a real caterpillar? Caterpillars hatch from eggs laid by a butterfly or moth. What do they use to move? Although they have legs they do not use them for walking, but for clasping on to food and stalks. Caterpillars crawl along using their many muscles. Why are caterpillars difficult to find (camouflage)? For food they eat the leaves or fruit on which they have hatched. As they increase in size they shed their skins several times. Eventually, when they have eaten enough and are fully grown, they spin a cocoon round themselves and rest while their body is changing.

What to do

Let the children choose a place in the room where their 'caterpillar' is going to feed. The size of the area (and the amount of 'food' available) will determine the size of the caterpillar to be made. Cut the egg cartons to make a small caterpillar or join sections together (with the stapler) to make a longer one. Using the metal skewer, carefully make holes on either side of the head ready for the feelers/antennae (see diagram). Choose the colour needed to paint the caterpillar so that it will blend in with the background of its 'feeding' place. It may be necessary to mix the paints to obtain the right colour. When the paint is dry, thread the pipe-cleaner into one of the holes and out of the other to make the feelers. Stick on two buttons or bits of felt to serve as eyes. Place the caterpillar in its selected spot where it will be camouflaged.

Follow-up activities

✧ Can the children find each other's caterpillars against the camouflage?
✧ Look for the holes in some home-grown cabbage leaves.
✧ Compare the different lengths of the egg-carton caterpillars. How many segments do they each have?
✧ Ask the children to crawl along the floor like a caterpillar, squashing themselves up then stretching out again.
✧ Make a temporary home for caterpillars in a jar, with holes pierced in the lid. Add some twigs. After a couple of days of observation, release the caterpillars where they were found.
✧ Read *The Very Hungry Caterpillar* by Eric Carle (Puffin).
✧ Sing the rhyme 'Little Arabella Miller' from *This Little Puffin* compiled by Elizabeth Matterson (Puffin).
✧ Sing the song 'Caterpillar' on page 87 of the Resources section.

BUTTERFLY BLOBS

Objective

Art – To use paint and paper to create symmetrically-patterned butterfly wings.

Group size

Six children.

What you need

A large piece of coloured sugar paper for each child, pencils, scissors, powder-paint, ready-mix or fluorescent paint, brushes.

Preparation

Fold the paper in half and draw the outline of a butterfly wing up to the fold as shown in the

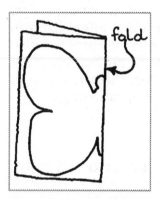

illustration. Cut round the folded outline and unfold the paper to show two wings. One butterfly is needed for each child.

What to do

Give each child a paper butterfly (older children may be able to make their own) and ask them to fold one wing back under the other (back to how it was when you cut it out). Let the children choose which paint they want to 'blob' on to the one wing to make a pattern. Make sure they don't brush it across the paper. Now they can carefully bring out the other wing from underneath and fold it on top of the blobs they have made. Show them how to smooth gently over the top wing with their hands. This will squeeze the paint blobs between the two wings. Unfold the butterfly to show the symmetrical pattern on both wings. Leave the butterfly open to dry.

Discussion

While a caterpillar is inside its cocoon it is changing into a pupa. Who can guess what crawls out of the cocoon when the pupa has fully grown? At first the butterfly is damp and soft and hangs from a stem to dry out and wait for its wings to stiffen. Do the children know what a butterfly is looking for when it flies away? It lands on a brightly-coloured flower and can detect whether there is any nectar (a sweet sugary liquid) inside the flower. Butterflies often fly to flowers which are the same colour as they are. Can the children think why a butterfly would do this?

Follow-up activities

✧ Tuck one of your butterfly wings underneath the other and hold the straight edge of the patterned wing up against a mirror. What can you see?
✧ Decorate the underneath of your butterfly wings with green blobs to make them blend in with the leaves.
✧ Flap your arms like butterfly wings. Raise your 'wings' above your head like a butterfly does when it's asleep.
✧ How many words can you make from the word BUTTERFLY?
✧ Make a 'blob' moth. It has much duller colours than a butterfly and rests with its wings flat.
✧ Say the rhyme 'Butterfly Butterfly' by Jan Betts, from *Knock at the Door* (Ward Lock).
✧ Make some butterfly cakes.

JELLY AND TADPOLES

Objective

English – A handwriting activity to improve pencil control and to familiarise children with full stops and commas.

Group size

Eight children.

What you need

Real frog-spawn but if this is not possible pictures of frog-spawn, tadpoles and frogs. Provide for each child: a small irregularly-shaped piece of bubble wrap, an indelible black pen, a pencil and a piece of paper.

What to do

Invite the children to look at the frog-spawn and if necessary point out the jelly-like substance which surrounds every black egg. Give each child a piece of bubble wrap and a black pen, for marking a black dot in the middle of each bubble so that it resembles frog-spawn. Explain to the children how they can avoid smudging by moving the bubble wrap round as they draw the dots. Show them a picture of some tadpoles and let them draw tadpole shapes on a piece of paper. Help the younger children by drawing some heads first to which they can just add the tails. Suggest that they curve the tadpole tails in different directions. Ask the children to find full stops and commas (like eggs and tadpoles) in their reading books and explain to them how they are used.

Discussion

After the children have looked at the frog-spawn, let them touch it gently if they want to. What does it feel like? When frogs have laid their spawn they leave it floating in pond water until it hatches. In a couple of days the eggs start to change their shape and grow longer. The tadpoles have a head and body all in one and can soon wriggle out of the jelly. How can tadpoles swim before their legs have grown? The tadpole's tail starts to shrink as soon as its legs begin to grow. What are tadpoles called when they have four legs, no tail and can leap?

Follow-up activities

✧ Make a jelly to eat. Just as it is setting, add a few currants to look like eggs in spawn.

✧ Make some Plasticine models of tadpoles. Bend some tails to the right and some tails to the left.

✧ Try this tongue twister – 'Ten tiny tadpoles try to touch their tails'.

✧ Keep some frog-spawn in a large glass bowl of pond water. Add some pond plants for the tadpoles to eat and some stones for them to hide under. Return the tadpoles back to a pond before their tails completely disappear and they start jumping out by themselves! Remember to give them extra food – goldfish food will do.

✧ Read the poem 'The Tadpole' on page 70 of the Resources section.

✧ Sing the song 'Tadpole' on page 88 of the Resources section.

LEAP FROG

Objective

PE – To move in different ways which relate to the stages in the life cycle of a frog.

Group size

The whole group.

What you need

If it is early spring, bring in some frog-spawn and a bowl of tadpoles. If this is not possible then pictures will do and also a picture of a frog.

Discussion

Let the children look at the picture of the frog and ask them to describe it. Do they notice that its skin is smooth and shiny, its eyes are large and bulge out, its feet are webbed and its back legs are much longer than its front legs? Why do they think that a frog needs such long back legs? Stress that they use them for leaping as well as swimming. A frog is a land and water animal and needs to stay damp. What would happen if it became too dry? (It would die.) A frog uses its short front legs for putting slugs or worms into its mouth. It can flick its sticky tongue out very quickly to catch insects to eat. Discuss with the children how a frog develops from a tadpole and how a tadpole starts off as an egg in frog-spawn.

What to do

Ask the children to show the three main stages of a frog's life cycle by moving in different ways. Let them work something out for themselves. If they need help, arrange them into groups to act as blobs of frog-spawn, link their arms together and show them how to wobble! They can drift around the room in their wobbly groups, just like frog-spawn floating around a pond. Soon one or two can start to wriggle away from the group and swim around using one arm like a tadpole's tail. When they have all changed into tadpoles they can gradually start to 'grow' their limbs until they have four legs and no tail. Crouching like frogs, they can leap from lily-pads to rocks and then on to land. Here they will find slugs, worms and insects. They may also

hide under stones to protect themselves from larger animals.

Follow-up activities

◇ The children can draw the stages of a frog's life cycle in a large circle (as shown in the illustration).
◇ Compare a toad to a frog. A toad has a dry, rough, warty skin and short back legs.
◇ Sing 'Five Little Freckled Frogs' by Jan Betts from *Knock at the Door* (Ward Lock).
◇ A frogman is a person who works under water wearing a wet suit and flippers and using breathing equipment. Draw a frogman in an underwater scene.
◇ Say the rhyme 'Frogs jump' from *Up, Up and Away* by Derek Pearson (OUP).
◇ Make a pond life display (see Chapter 7).

CRACK AN EGG

Objective

Science – To examine a hen's egg both outside and inside and to consider its suitability as an environment for a chick to develop.

Group size

Six children.

What you need

Three eggs – two raw and one hard-boiled, a large glass bowl, a jug of cold water, a thermos flask of boiling water, a straining spoon, at least one magnifying glass.

What to do

Allow the children to handle one of the uncooked eggs in its shell (hold it over the glass bowl just in case). Ask them to try to break the shell by squeezing it hard with *one* hand (it's impossible to break it).

Half fill the bowl with cold water and crack the egg into it. Give the children a magnifying glass to find a little dot on the yolk. Most shop eggs have white dots, a red dot means that a little chick would have started to grow (both are safe to eat). Use the spoon to strain off the cold water.

Pour boiling water slowly over the egg and watch the 'white' and yolk. Put the remaining two eggs on the table and guess which one is cooked. Spin both eggs on the table top. The uncooked one will spin more slowly and unevenly. Examine the broken eggshell to find the air pocket at one end. Peel the hard-boiled egg and look for a similar air pocket.

Discussion

Why is the eggshell so strong? Explain that it needs to be tough to protect a growing chick and also to take the weight of a mother bird sitting on it to keep it warm.

When the egg was cracked into the cold water did the children see that the jelly floated and spread white threads into the water? Did they notice that the yolk floated in its own bag inside the jelly? Can the children guess what a chick feeds on while it is growing inside the egg? (The yolk.) Where does the chick get air from? (The air pocket.)

A new chick is able to walk straight away and peck for seeds and worms to eat. In what way is this different from a human baby? When the two eggs were spun on the table, what made one spin more slowly and unevenly?

Follow-up activities

◇ Make some meringues.
◇ Sing 'Humpty Dumpty Sat on a Wall'.
◇ Use food dye in the water when you hard-boil eggs. Decorate the coloured eggs with felt-tipped pens.
◇ Look at an empty bird's nest then try to make one from some straw and mud.
◇ Compare the size and weight of a duck and a goose egg to that of a hen's egg.
◇ Say the poem 'Eggs for breakfast' from *The Book of a Thousand Poems* (Collins).

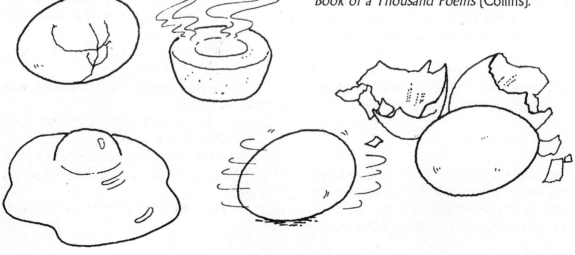

·INCEY WINCEY

Objective

Religious Education – To encourage the children not to give up, even when faced with difficulties.

Group size

Six children.

What you need

Pictures of spiders and webs, a pair of scissors. For each child: a piece of card with holes punched in it (see below), blunt-ended needles and thick black thread.

Preparation

Cut a piece of card approximately 15cm square. Draw some lines (like spokes in a wheel) on the card and place it on a piece of carpet. Use a sharp instrument to punch holes through the card into the carpet at set intervals along these lines (as shown in the illustration). You will need one card and a threaded needle for each child. Make a large knot at one end of the thread (which does not need to be too long).

What to do

Sing together the nursery rhyme 'Incey Wincey Spider Climbed up the Spout' (both verses). Look at the pictures of spiders and webs and point out how the spoke pattern looks like a bicycle wheel. Give each child their own card and threaded needle and show them how to make stitches in and out of the holes. It doesn't matter if the web gets to be a bit lop-sided or tangled - after all, young spiders who are learning how to spin may not have perfect webs!

When the children have finished sewing (they may want to use more than one thread), knot the ends and store the needles away carefully.

Discussion

Have the children ever struggled to do something, like the spider who was washed down the spout? Was it difficult for them to learn to dress themselves, ride their bikes or swim? Did they feel like giving

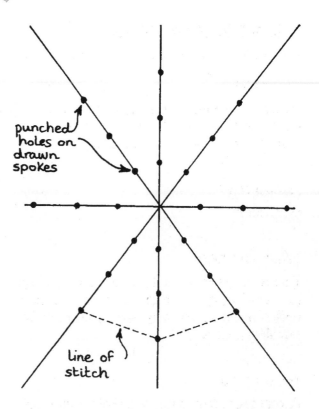

punched holes on drawn spokes

line of stitch

up? Have they ever watched a baby learning to walk? Although the baby keeps falling over it gets up and tries again and again, just like a spider.

Why do spiders spin webs? They eat insects that they have trapped. A spider can also spin a silk cocoon to protect its eggs. When some types of baby spiders have hatched, their mother carries them round on her back until they are old enough to look after themselves. Young spiders grow out of their skins as they get bigger, just like children who grow out of their clothes! Where do spiders like to hide?

Follow-up activity

✧ Draw a thick black spider on the sewn web card.
✧ Count how many legs a spider has. How many legs do two spiders have?
✧ Can the children scuttle across the floor very quickly just like a spider?
✧ Try to spot a spider's web sparkling with morning dew drops.
✧ Dip your finger in a little corn oil and then touch a spider's web. What happens?
✧ Say the action rhyme 'I Have a Little Spider' from *This Little Puffin* compiled by Elizabeth Matterson (Penguin).
✧ Sing 'Under a Web' from *Count Me In* (A & C Black).

DISCOVERING DINOSAURS

* *

Objective

History — To learn about creatures who lived many millions of years ago and to make a dinosaur picture.

Group size

Eight children.

What you need

Pictures of different types of dinosaur, an outline drawing of a dinosaur and half an eggshell for each child, a flat tray, pieces of conifer from a Leyland cyprus hedge or branches of a used Christmas tree, wax crayons, PVA glue and a spreader.

Preparation

Draw the dinosaur outline choosing a long or short body and tail, long or short front legs, horns or claws (based on illustrations of actual dinosaurs in reference books). Make a copy for each child. Thoroughly wash some used eggshells and bake them for an hour in a cool oven. Cut some tiny sprigs off the conifer branches.

What to do

Give each child a copy of the dinosaur sheet to colour in. When it's time to add the scaly skin, the children should first spread some glue over their dinosaur outline. Let each child have a turn at smashing half an eggshell with their fist into the flat tray. These bits of eggshell can now be scattered on to the dinosaur pictures to give a scale effect. Glue some conifer sprigs along the backbone of the dinosaur to look like sharp spikes.

Discussion

Show the children the pictures of dinosaurs. Do they think they look like any other animals? Dinosaurs lived more than 65 million years ago and some looked like crocodiles and lizards. We have learned about them from finding patterns of their bones in rocks (fossils). Explain that not all dinosaurs were enormous: Brachiosaurus was one of the biggest and was the size of a very large tree while Compsognathus was very small, about the size of a chicken. Can the children guess why some dinosaurs had horns, back plates (overlapping scales of armour) and spikes? Ask them if they think that dinosaur babies grew inside hard-shelled eggs. Mother dinosaurs brought food to their newly-hatched babies, who waited in nests in the sand. Which other animals grow up in nests?

Follow-up activities

✧ Write out the names of some dinosaurs. Ask the children to count the letters. Which one has the most letters?

✧ Some people believe that there is a monster living in Loch Ness. Find Scotland on a map.

✧ Dinosaurs used their tails to balance themselves. How do other animals use their tails. (Dogs, monkeys and squirrels, for example.)

✧ Make some pretend fossils by pressing different shapes into Plasticine, or salt-dough. Try using a key, a coin or a paperclip.

✧ Cut up a dinosaur outline then piece it back together again like dinosaur fossils were re-assembled.

✧ Draw your own type of monster and make up a long name for it.

✧ Sing the song 'Clomp! Stomp! Tromperty Tromp!' on page 83 of the Resources section.

THEMES
for early years

CHAPTER 3
SEEDS AND PLANTS

It is very hard for a child to realise that the plants they see all around them have grown from small seeds or from 'bits' of plants. This chapter gives children the opportunity to sow seeds and watch plants growing from them. They will see that plants need water, warmth and light just as much as they themselves do.

FROM SMALL BEGINNINGS

Objectives

Art – To note that seeds are different shapes, sizes and colours; to make a seed collage on a plate.

Group size

Six children.

What you need

A paper side plate for each child, pencils, PVA glue and spreaders, a collection of different seeds (dried peas, kidney beans, black-eyed beans, pumpkin seeds, mustard seeds, peppercorns, wheat grain, sunflower seeds, rice, bird seeds, apple pips, conkers and acorns).

What to do

Let the children handle and experiment with the different types of seeds, arranging them in different patterns on their plates before deciding on their final arrangement.

If they decide on a random pattern, they can spread the glue thickly all over the surface of the plate and then sprinkle on a mixture of seeds and press them into the glue with their fingertips.

If they want a more orderly pattern, they should glue only a small area of the plate at a time. Start with a patch in the middle, add one type of seed, press them into the glue and shake off the surplus. Now glue another small section or a circular area around the central patch and add another type of seed. Repeat this until the plate is covered with seeds and leave it flat until the glue has dried.

Discussion

Explain to the children that the seeds they have been handling all come from flowering plants. The seeds would grow into new plants if given the right conditions. The wheat grain would grow into wheat (a type of corn), and the dried bean into a bean plant. Each type of flowering plant has its own particular seeds. What type of seed does an apple tree have? Compare the difference between an apple pip and the seed (stone) that comes from a peach or plum tree. Seeds need some type of covering to protect them from drying out or being crushed. Why does a conker (horse chestnut seed) have a prickly case? (To stop animals eating it.)

NB Make sure the children do not try to eat the seeds, and warn them about the dangers of choking.

Follow-up activities

◇ Hang up the seed collages. Punch two holes in the plate rim and make a hanging loop with some thin nylon string.
◇ Put the leftover seeds into tight-lidded pots to make shakers. Which shakers make the most noise?
◇ Put ten seeds of the same type touching each other in a row. Do the same with other types of seeds. Arrange the rows underneath each other for comparison. Which seeds make the longest row?
◇ Count and weigh 20 dried peas and 20 butter beans. Which are the heaviest?
◇ Cut open two apples, extract the seeds and see if the apples have the same amount of pips.
◇ Sing the song 'A seed' on page 87 of the Resources section.

SEEDS MOVE HOME

Objective

Physical Education – To illustrate the different methods of seed dispersal (wind, animal and explosion) by miming and moving in a variety of ways.

Group size

The whole group.

What you need

It is preferable to provide the following natural products but as this may not always be possible alternatives are suggested: a dried poppy head on its stalk or a pepper pot filled with dry sand; sycamore seeds or a small strip of lightweight paper (approx. 2cm × 15cm); a dandelion 'clock' or a tin of baby powder; dried pea or bean pods, or a can of fizzy drink.

Discussion

When seeds are ripe they leave their parent plant to grow into new plants. What would happen if all the seeds started to grow in the same place? Some seeds can travel a long way from the parent plant so that they don't have to compete for light and water. Can the children suggest ways in which the seeds travel? The wind helps move dandelion seeds which float like parachutes, sycamore seeds spin through the air like helicopters, a poppy head scatters its tiny seeds as the wind blows it backwards and forwards. How do animals help to move seeds? Birds eat fruit and then get rid of the seeds in their droppings, squirrels hide nuts to eat later and then forget where they are hidden. Guess what happens to the seeds and the hidden nuts. As vegetable pods ripen they dry out, explode and scatter the seeds.

What to do

Show the children how the poppy would move in the wind, shaking its head and scattering seeds (or shake sand from the pepper pot into the air). Bang the baby powder container on to a hard surface and compare the powder that drifts out to how dandelion 'clock' seeds blow away in the wind. Drop the sycamore seed or paper strip from a height and watch it spin in the air. How is this like a helicopter?

For the movement session, the children can choose whether to shake, drift or spin in the way that seeds do in the wind. They can move like birds and squirrels do, eating, dropping and hiding nuts. Remind them how animals act when they hear a sudden noise and are frightened.

Pull open the bean or pea pods (or the fizzy drink can) and let the children make the same bursting movements as seeds which fly out of pods.

Follow-up activities

✧ The children can work in pairs and take it in turns to guess which type of seed dispersal their partner is miming.
✧ Sing and play 'Here We Go Gathering Nuts in May' (traditional).
✧ Hang a pine cone outside and watch it open in dry weather to let its seeds drop. It will also tell you when it's going to rain.
✧ Sing the song 'Dandelion clock' on page 84 of the Resources section.
✧ Say the poem 'The acorn' from *The Book of a Thousand Poems* (Collins).

ROOTS AND SHOOTS

Objective

Science – To grow a bean, examine its parts and see that roots grow down and shoots grow up.

Group size

Six children.

What you need

A very tall glass jar, damp sand, a tablespoon, two paper towels, a magnifying glass, four dry broad beans, a jug of water, a label and pencil, an adult's sock.

Preparation

Twenty-four hours before the activity, soak two of the dry broad beans in cold water.

What to do

Let the children compare the two dry and the two soaked beans.

Line the inside of the jar with the two dry paper towels. Spoon the sand down inside the paper (almost to the top) to hold it in place. Using the spoon handle, ease two spaces (on opposite sides) between the side of the jar and the paper. Position the two soaked beans in these spaces, one vertically and one horizontally with the tip uppermost as shown in the illustration. Pour a little water carefully down the sides of the jar to wet the sand and paper lining. Use the label to record the starting date and cover the jar with the sock.

Examine the beans every day, noting any changes that take place. When the beans have sprouted (in about three days' time), remove the sock and continue observing the seeds. Make sure that the lining paper is always damp.

Discussion

Ask the children to describe the differences between the dry and the soaked beans. Why have the soaked beans become fatter? Can they guess what will happen to the beans which are covered by the sock? After a week, when green leaves are showing, ask what has happened to the seed covers. Although

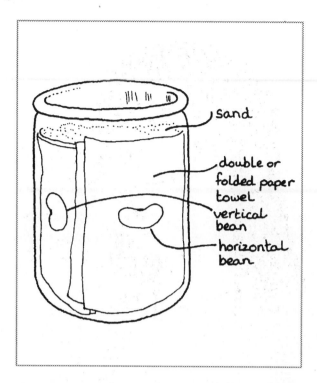

sand
double or folded paper towel
vertical bean
horizontal bean

the beans are in different positions, in which direction are both white roots growing? (Down towards the earth – due to gravity.) What are the green bean shoots growing up towards? (The light.) Why does the main root have lots of little roots growing from it? Root hairs help the plant to drink lots of water. If the beans had been planted in soil, what do the children think the hidden roots would look like?

Follow-up activities

✧ Display a record of the growing bean (see Chapter 7).

✧ Plant the growing bean in the garden and let it climb up a cane.

✧ Soak some dried butter beans overnight. Next day, give each one a squeeze and watch it pop out of its cover.

✧ Carefully separate the two halves of a soaked bean. Look through a magnifying glass at the flat side of each half. The tiny shoot sticks out like a tail and the root has left its imprint inside the other half.

✧ How many do two halves make when they are put back together?

✧ Sing and dance to 'Oats and Beans and Barley Grow' from *Oranges and Lemons* compiled by Karen King (OUP).

✧ Say the poem 'The bean seed' on page 74 of the Resources section.

GROWING NEEDS

Objective

Science — To discover that seeds need water, warmth and light to grow into healthy plants.

Group size

Twelve children.

What you need

100g mixed birdseed bought from a pet shop, four shallow bowls (dessert dishes), two plates to completely cover the top of the dishes, eight paper towels, cling-film, a jug of water, some labels and a pencil.

What to do

Place one paper towel on top of another, fold the towels into quarters and put them into the bottom of a bowl. Wet the towels and pour off any excess water. Repeat this for all four of the bowls and sprinkle half a teaspoonful of seeds into each. Cover two of the dishes with the plates and the other two with some cling-film. Place one plate-covered dish and one film-covered dish inside a fridge. Place the other two dishes in a warm room in good light. Label each dish with the starting date and the place where it is kept. Look at the seeds every day for two weeks and note down what is happening to them — size, colour, direction of growth. When you look at the seeds under the plates, replace the plates quickly to stop light getting to them. Ensure that the paper towels are kept damp all the time.

Discussion

Ask the children why the birdseeds weren't growing when they were bought from the shop. What do seeds need to grow into healthy plants? There is just the right amount of food in the seed itself for it to sprout into a seedling. In three or four days the seeds under the plate in the warm place will be longer than those under the cling-film. Seeds like to sprout in the dark. Which seedlings look healthiest after a week? Once seeds have sprouted they need light to grow green leaves. If they are kept in the dark for too long they will grow yellow and straggly as they search for light. What has happened to the two dishes of seeds in the fridge? Seeds will not start to grow if they are not warm enough.

Follow-up activities

✧ What happens to seeds which do not have enough air to grow? Fill a bowl, in which seeds are planted, with water, and cover it with a plate in a warm room. Do the seeds sprout?
✧ Draw a face on half an empty eggshell. Fill it with damp kitchen paper. Sprinkle on some mustard seeds. In a few days your shell face will have hair on top. (See illustration above.)
✧ Sometimes seeds do not have baby plants inside them. Put ten mustard seeds in-between two damp paper towels and cover them with a plate. How many seeds have sprouted by the end of a week?
✧ Say the action poem 'A seedy story' on page 71 of the Resources section.
✧ Sing the action rhyme 'The cherry tree' from *Round and Round the Garden* by Sarah Williams (OUP).

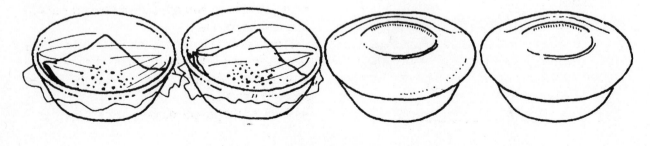

SIZING STEMS

Objective

Mathematics – To measure the heights of different plants and to order things according to size.

Group size

Six children.

What you need

A vase of mixed flowers of different colours, some paper towels, a large piece of paper, narrow strips (about 3cm wide) of white paper at least the length of the tallest flower, scissors and a pencil for each child, wax crayons, glue and spreaders.

What to do

Dry the stems and give each child a flower and a strip of paper. Show them how to lay the flower on top of the paper strip and to mark the length of the stem with a pencil (from one end of the strip up to but not including the flower head), as shown in the illustration above. Move the flower away, then cut the paper off above the mark and throw

mark length of stem

cut away this part of paper

away the extra bit of paper. Use a crayon to colour the remaining strip (which is the length of the stem) green or another suitable colour. When all the flowers have been measured, put them back into the vase of water. Let the children arrange the paper strip 'stems' in size order, starting with either the shortest or longest. Glue these ordered strips on to the large piece of paper. Label the display 'The size of our flower stems' and pin it up on the wall.

Discussion

Explain to the children that a stem is part of the shoot which grows upwards from a seed. What is a stem for? As well as holding flower heads for insects to visit, a stem also supports the leaves of a plant. Stems stop growing when they have reached a certain height, depending on the type of plant – just like people stop growing taller when they are grown-up. How does food and water travel from the underground roots to the leaves and flowers? They are sucked up the stem like juice being sucked up through a drinking straw. Do the children know why some stems are prickly? (To avoid being eaten and damaged.) Who knows what the stem of a tree is called? Bushes have lots of woody stems. Soft green stems die back each year but tree trunks and bushes live for years and years.

Follow-up activities

✧ Make flower heads to stick on to the stems.
✧ Cut the top 3cm from a stick of celery and keep this piece wrapped and moist. Make a clean cut at the base of the remaining stick and stand it in 6cm of red coloured water (use food dye). After four hours, cut the stick in half and compare the inside to the wrapped piece.
✧ Stand two children back to back. Who is the tallest and who is the shortest of the pair?
✧ Sing 'The sunflower song' on page 86 of the Resources section.
✧ What is the opposite of long, up, old, dark, hot?

THIRSTY ROOTS

Objective

Science — To watch roots growing and discover their function.

Group size

The whole group.

What you need

Three onions of approximately the same size, two tall glasses or vases with narrow necks, a plant pot with bulb fibre or compost, a jug of water, labels and a pencil, a piece of ivy with its roots.

What to do

Let the children handle the onion bulbs and point out the dried-up root fibres at the base.

Pour enough water into one of the tall glasses so that when a bulb is placed in the neck of the glass it is only just slightly above the surface. Put the second bulb into the neck of the other glass which contains no water. Make a small depression in the bulb fibre in the plant pot, dampen it and then sit the third bulb in it. Label each container with the date on which you start the experiment.

The roots of the bulb in the glass of water should start to grow within two or three days. Keep a record of what happens to the three bulbs. If the water in the glass starts to smell, change it carefully without damaging the bulb's roots. Ensure that the bulb fibre is kept damp.

After about two weeks, when you can see the roots growing strongly in the glass, gently lift the bulb which is growing in the plant pot and examine its roots. Compare the roots of the three bulbs.

Look at the roots growing on the piece of ivy. Are they similar to the roots on the bulbs?

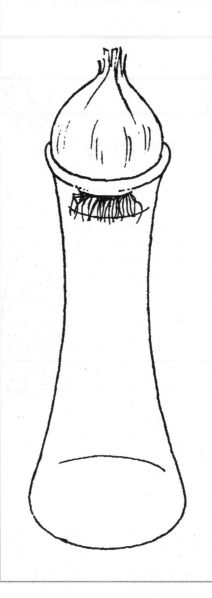

Discussion

Talk about the different rates of growth of the three bulbs. Ask the children why one didn't grow at all. Plant roots normally grow underground so how can you tell if their roots have no water? (The plant wilts.)

Tree roots are very strong. They branch out, and can push through hard earth to find water and food (minerals in the soil). If there is something in their way, they will either grow round it or push through it.

Have the children ever seen cracked or lifted paving stones around the base of a tree? Why else do tree roots need to be very strong? (To anchor the tree and prevent it from being blown over.)

What helps ivy to cling to walls or tree trunks as it grows? Compare ivy roots to people's fingers or cats' claws.

Follow-up activities

◇ Use the photocopiable sheet on page 92 and ask the children to draw roots growing towards water. They can use a thick crayon to do this.

◇ Dramatise the story of 'The Enormous Turnip' on page 77 of the Resources section.

◇ Cut through a bulb (use daffodil, tulip or crocus bulbs) lengthwise and look at the arrangement of the layers.

◇ Slice across the middle of an onion and count the rings. (Remember your handkerchief!)

LEAVES HAVE VEINS

Objective

Art – To make leaf prints and notice the different sizes, shapes and textures of leaves.

Group size

Six children.

What you need

A collection of at least six different types of leaves (such as laurel, ivy, beech, cabbage, fern, conifer), six different-coloured paints ready-mixed in pots with a brush in each, a large piece of painting paper for each child, a pile of newspaper pages cut in half, a wastepaper bin, a damp cloth.

What to do

Let each child choose a leaf and a paint colour (they can all swap round later). Show them how to place their leaf with the vein side facing upwards on to a piece of newspaper and then paint the surface of the leaf using the brush. Place this leaf with the painted side down on to the painting paper. Put another piece of newspaper on top of the leaf and carefully rub your hand over it so that the leaf imprint will be left on the painting paper. Throw away the used pieces of newspaper and let the children repeat the process with the different leaves, making prints on to the same piece of paper. Be careful not to smudge! If necessary, use the damp cloth to wipe hands.

Discussion

Allow the children to examine some (unpainted) leaves and discuss the different sizes and shapes. Point out that they all have veins, which can often be seen more clearly on the underside. Although plants take in food through their roots in the soil, they need other types of food to grow strong and healthy. Leaves are very important to plants because they are able to make food using air and water during daylight. How does this food reach the other parts of the plant? The leaf veins can carry food around in much the same way as the blood in our veins. Some leaves are shiny, others are very pointed, but all are made in such a way that rain

runs off them. If it didn't it would block the leaf's pores (invisible openings) and stop the plant being able to breathe.

Follow-up activities

✧ Arrange some leaf prints to form a pattern sequence.
✧ Use different shades of green paint to give leaf prints a 'natural' look.
✧ Sort leaves into sets according to type, size, shape, dark or light colour.
✧ Leaves grow very thickly in a jungle. How would the children move if they had to hack their way through?
✧ Compare the edges of leaves. Staple a leaf to a piece of paper and draw round its edge with a pencil.
✧ Can the children find the veins on their hands?
✧ Sing the song 'Falling leaves' from *Count Me In* (A & C Black).

NEW PLANTS FROM OLD

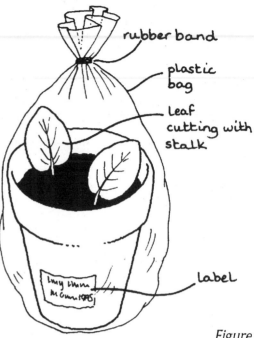

Figure 1

Objective

Science – To grow new plants by cutting off pieces from plants that are already growing.

Group size

Six children.

What you need

Two sprouting potatoes, a magnifying glass, a sharp knife and a cutting board, a bag of all-purpose compost, six 10cm plant pots, six labels, pencils, a tray, a jug of water.

Preparation

Five or six weeks before you are ready to do this activity put two 'old' potatoes (with tough thick skins) in a cool, light (not sunny) room until they sprout white shoots of about 1cm in length.

What to do

Allow the children to look at the potatoes through the magnifying glass but don't handle them too much or the white shoots will be knocked off. Ask the children to cut a potato into three pieces, each containing at least one shoot or 'eye'. (Supervise the use of the sharp knife at all times.) Half-fill each plant pot with compost and lay a potato piece on top of each. Cover this cutting with more compost and press it down gently so that it settles 2cm below the rim of the pot. Tell the children to write their own name and the date on a label before sticking it to their pot. Water the pots and leave them on the tray on a window-sill. Keep the compost moist at all times. The shoots should appear within a week and the leaves four days after that.

Discussion

All plants grow from seeds but some plants can make new plants without the need for seeds. They can grow a new plant from a piece of themselves, such as part of a stem or a root. Potatoes can be grown in this way. Have the children ever seen any plants growing baby plants? Strawberry plants send out long thin stems across the ground called runners. A new young strawberry plant will grow on the end of a runner. Buttercups spread in this way and can become a real nuisance. Daffodil bulbs grow baby bulbs around themselves to make new plants. Raspberry plants send out very long shoots underground. These 'suckers' grow into new plants.

Follow-up activities

✧ Plant three African violet leaves (with stalks attached) into a pot of damp compost. Place the pot in a secured transparent plastic bag. (See Figure 1.) Leave it in a warm, light place until new plantlets start to grow after about five weeks. Remove the bag once they are growing well.
✧ Split a garlic bulb into little bulbs or cloves and count how many new plants would grow.
✧ Draw a picture of a garden covered in buttercups.
✧ Sing the song 'One potato, two potato' from *This Little Puffin* compiled by Elizabeth Matterson (Puffin).

CHAPTER 4
TREES AND FLOWERS

The seasons of the year affect all living things. Only during the warmer months of the year are the brightest coloured flowers seen. It is in autumn that some of the trees lose their leaves and by winter they are bare. The children will be able to watch these changes and gain an understanding of the importance of trees and flowers.

COUNT THE RINGS

Objective

History – To introduce children to the idea that a tree started growing a long time ago; to make rubbings of logs.

Group size

Six children.

What you need

Some pictures of different types and sizes of trees, some tree logs (with rough and smooth bark) of different diameters and which are split lengthwise, plenty of thin plain paper, drawing pins, short stubby wax crayons, thick soft pencils.

What to do

Look at the pictures of the trees and point out from which part of the trees the logs would be cut. Let the children feel the logs and bark (warn them about splinters). Count the rings or the lines on the different-shaped logs. Fix a piece of paper to each log with drawing pins. The children can use a soft pencil or the edge of a wax crayon to rub gently backwards and forwards until the lines of the wood show through, on to the paper. Each child can make a rubbing of a log cut crosswise and lengthwise.

Discussion

A tree is a large woody plant. What do trees start to grow from? An oak tree starts from a seed called an acorn, and a horse chestnut tree from a conker. It takes many years for a plant to grow from a young bendy-stemmed sapling to a tall stiff tree with branches and twigs. What is the thickest part of the tree called? The trunk grows a little bit fatter and taller each year as the tree grows. The circles or lines of wood inside the logs show how many years old the tree was. Why are trees so important? They help to give us clean air to breathe, stop the soil from being washed away by the rain, give us shelter from hot sun and from strong wind. Some trees are very beautiful, and have been growing for much longer that we have.

Follow-up activities

✧ Measure round some growing tree trunks with a piece of tape. Measure the tape against your height. Are you as tall as the tree is fat?
✧ Collect some fallen branches and twigs and lay them out in order of thickness.
✧ Look at an old mossy tree trunk through a magnifying glass – do you see anything moving?
✧ Make a collection of things to be found in the room which are made from wood.
✧ Bend and sway like a very young tree and then stand straight and stiff like a big old tree.
✧ Break some little twigs to the same length. Secure them round a thick piece of branch with a rubber band to make a little broom stick.
✧ Sing the song 'Count the rings' on page 81 of the Resources section.

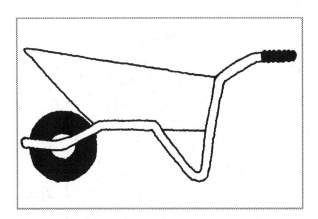

THE FOUR SEASONS

Objective

Geography — To encourage children to use their senses (not taste) in finding out how seasonal changes affect leaves; to make a picture of autumn leaves collected in a barrow.

Group size

Six children.

What you need

An outline drawing of an empty wheelbarrow for each child, crayons or felt-tipped pens, a variety of evergreen leaves, a bag full of autumn leaves, glue and spreaders.

Preparation

Draw the outline of a wheelbarrow (as shown in the illustration). Make a copy for each child on A4 paper.

What to do

Take the children into the garden to collect some fallen autumn leaves and put them into a wheelbarrow or a bin-bag. Show them places where they may pick some evergreen leaves safely. Once inside, let them examine both types of leaves and encourage them to feel them, listen to them and smell them. Give each child a copy of the wheelbarrow outline to colour, and then spread some glue in the area above it. Let them stick some of the fallen leaves on to the paper to make a picture of a barrow brimming with autumn leaves.

Discussion

Ask the children to describe the look and feel of both types of leaves, such as thick or thin, rough or smooth, shiny or prickly, tough or delicate, waxy or dull. Listen to both types of leaves as they handle them — is it only the dry leaves which rustle? Let them compare the smell of the autumn leaves to the smell of the green leaves. Explain that there are different times during the year called winter, spring, summer and autumn. In winter, when it is cold, some trees are bare and have no leaves at all. Once the weather gets warmer, leaf buds start to grow and the trees and hedges start to turn green. By summer, when there is more daylight, the buds have burst out into new leaves. As the days get colder and shorter, the soft flat leaves from some trees change colour and start to drop off on to the ground. That's when we tidy them up into a wheelbarrow!

Follow-up activities

✧ Drag your feet through autumn leaves and listen to the sound they make.
✧ In spring, put a horse chestnut twig in a vase of water and watch the 'sticky buds' open out.
✧ Pack some autumn leaves into a bin-bag. Leave the bag sealed for a few months then open it up to see how the leaves have broken down into compost.
✧ Fill a vase with a collection of evergreen leaves. Paint a picture of the different shapes and shades of green.

TREE LIFE

❖❖❖❖❖❖❖❖❖❖❖❖❖❖❖❖❖❖❖❖❖❖❖❖❖❖❖❖

Objective

English – To listen to verbal clues and, in response, match creature picture cards to the animal names on a tree outline.

Group size

Six children.

What you need

A copy of photocopiable sheet on page 93 for each child, crayons, scissors.

Preparation

Cut out the five separate picture cards on the photocopiable sheets.

What to do

Give a copy of the tree outline and the five picture cards to each child. Read through the creature names on the picture cards and the tree outline with the children. Tell them that you will give them 'clues' to help them to guess which creature, or thing, lives on or under a tree. When they think they know the answer to your clue they should pick a card and match it to the same word on the tree. After they have matched all the cards they can remove them and colour in the tree.

Possible clues to use with the photocopiable sheet include:

❖ *A long thin creature with no legs that wriggles through the soil.* (A worm.)
❖ *A bird that likes to fly at night.* (An owl.)
❖ *An animal with a long furry tail that jumps from branch to branch.* (A squirrel.)
❖ *A place where birds lay their eggs.* (A nest.)
❖ *A creature that is very good at spinning.* (A spider.)

Discussion

Trees provide shelter and food for many different animals. Owls are birds which hunt for food at night and like to eat mice. They perch high up in trees and are able to see in the dark. What sound do owls make? How do birds manage to build their nests? Why do they build them in the branches of trees? Baby birds are safe from creatures which live on the ground but what other dangers might there be in the nests? Worms pull dead leaves with them as they wriggle through the soil. The dead leaves decompose and provide food for growing trees and plants. A squirrel eats nuts from trees. Sometimes they spoil the tree's bark. What body parts do squirrels use to jump from tree to tree? Spiders spin silky webs which are so sticky that flies and other insects stick to them. What does a spider do with insects once they are trapped?

Follow-up activities

❖ How many different types of birds can the children spot resting on the trees outside?
❖ Think of other tree creatures and draw them on the tree outline (woodlice, slugs, snails, mice).
❖ Make a wormery in a large glass jar, by layering soil, leaves and sand. Add some worms then keep the jar covered – except when you have a quick look. You can tell if the worms have moved because the soil, sand and leaves will be all mixed up.
❖ Draw the outline shapes of different trees.
❖ Say the poem 'Forgiven' from *Now We Are Six* by A. A. Milne (Methuen).

PRETTY PETALS

Objective

Design and Technology — To design and create a flower arrangement on a summer greetings card.

Group size

Six children.

What you need

Three different types of flowers with large single heads (one bell-shaped, one with a flat head and one rose), sheets of paper of different colours and textures, a piece of card (approximate size A4) for each child, scissors and a pencil for each child, three pots of glue and six spreaders, felt-tipped pens.

Preparation

Fold all the pieces of card in half.

What to do

Show the children the three real flowers and encourage them to design their own. Ask them to choose a sheet of paper in a particular texture and colour, and show them how to fold it into quarters. To make the petals, they can draw two petal shapes on the top piece of the folded paper. Holding all the layers of paper together they then cut round these shapes. They can cut more petals in another colour to make a flower using two colours or to make more flowers. When they have decided how many petals they want to use for their flower head, they should arrange and glue them on to their own piece of folded card.

Some children may like to share their petals with friends and create flowers with multi-coloured heads. If they have left a gap in the middle of their flower they can coloured it in with a felt-tipped pen.

The finished work can be used as cards to give someone.

Discussion

Did the real flower petals overlap or fit into each other? Were all the petals on each flower the same shape and size? Why do the children think that some flowers are so brightly-coloured and have such a sweet perfume? Insects and some birds are attracted by colour and smell. Butterflies, wasps, flies and bees visit flowers and drink the sweet nectar. As they 'nose' around the petals to find nectar, their bodies brush against pollen grains which they then take to the next flowers they visit. This causes seeds to grow. Some flowers only give out their scent when it is dark. Moths who fly at night can't see the bright colours of flowers but can still find where the nectar is because they are guided by the flower's sweet perfume.

Follow-up activities

✧ Choose who you will give your summer card to. Write 'from —————' inside.

✧ Brush your fingers across the pollen stalks in the middle of a tulip or a lily. What is left on your fingers? (Take care with any children who might suffer from allergies.)

✧ Does the perfume of carnation-scented soap smell the same as a real carnation?

✧ Press some real flowers. Use flat-headed types and place them between sheets of newspaper. Pile some heavy books on top and leave for two weeks after which the flowers will be ready.

✧ Say the action poem 'Garden rainbow' on page 68 of the Resources section.

✧ Say the poem 'Pussy willows' from *Seeing and Doing New Anthology* (Thames Television).

BEAUTIFUL BLOSSOM

Objective

Art – To see how flowers of one type are all exactly the same and to finger-paint a blossom picture.

Group size

Six children.

What you need

A branch of blossom from an apple or another blossom tree, six light twigs about 25cm in length, adhesive tape, a piece of background paper (A4) in a soft shade for each child, three or four pots of paints ready-mixed in white and shades of pink, a saucer for each paint colour, a damp cloth.

Preparation

Fix a twig in the middle of each sheet of paper with two pieces of adhesive tape.

What to do

Point out to the children how the blossom grows in different shades of the same colour. Pour some paint out of each pot into a saucer. Show the children how to point with their index finger and then to dab the fingertip into a saucer of paint. By pressing their fingertip gently on to the paper, on either side of the twig, they can randomly 'finger-print' some blossom (as shown in the illustration). When the paint on their finger has been used up they can wipe their finger on the damp cloth and then dip it into another shade of paint. Let them also try using their thumbs to print.

Discussion

Blossom is made up of masses of little flowers which all look the same and grow in clusters on tree branches. The flowers on fruit trees are called blossom. Can the children think of the names of some of these fruit trees? (Apple, pear, plum, peach.) Blossom is very delicate and falls easily off tree branches in a strong wind. When lots of pale pink and white blossom floats down from the trees what does it look like? When the blossom has fallen the tree starts to grow fruit.

Some trees do not have blossom but have different types of flowers called catkins. These are soft spiky flowers which hang from trees such as willow and hazel. They are not brightly coloured because they do not need insects to move their pollen, the wind does it for them.

Follow-up activities

✧ Arrange the children's blossom branches all together to make a blossoming tree.
✧ Find a catkin and stick it on to a small outline drawing of a squirrel. It will look like a furry tail.
✧ Count how many clusters of blossom there are on one branch of a fruit tree.
✧ Orange blossom grows in hot countries such as Israel and South Africa. Find these places on a map of the world.
✧ Sing 'Think of a world without any flowers' from *Someone's Singing, Lord* (A & C Black).
✧ Read the poem 'Apple blossoms' in *The Book of a Thousand Poems* (Collins).

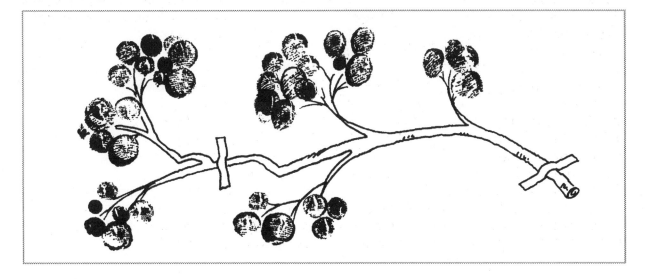

LAZY DAISY

Objective

English – To find out about flowers which grow wild and to work out their names from clues given as riddles.

Group size

Six children.

What you need

A list of riddles describing wild flowering plants (see below), some pictures of wild flowers as given in the riddles.

Preparation

Compile a list of riddles similar to the ones given below:

I'm thinking of a flower which rhymes with lazy, it grows in the grass because it's a ... [Daisy]
On the edge of the wood there's a lovely smell, everywhere I look there's another ... [Bluebell]
It starts with an 'r' as everyone knows, it feels very prickly because it's a ... [Rose]

Two children were lost called Hansel and Gretel, I hope they weren't stung by a stinging ... [Nettle]
Its purple leaves are as light as a feather, it brings good luck and its name is ... [Heather]

What to do

Show the children the pictures of wild flowers. Read out the riddles to the children and see who is able to guess the answers.

Discussion

Weeds are plants which grow wild in places where they are not meant to grow. Can the children suggest places where weeds would not be welcome? They grow very quickly and thickly and can sometimes be a real nuisance. Why don't farmers like weeds? Some farmers spray their fields with chemicals so that their crops can grow without being choked by weeds. Wild flowers are disappearing because of this poison. Some weeds, which grow under hedges and in fields or woods, are left to flower but people are not supposed to pick these wild flowers.

If grass is not cut and is left to grow wild, it will grow its own flowers. These pale green fluffy flowers are blown in the wind and their pollen flies into the air. This is what gives people hay fever and makes them sneeze.

Daisies are weeds that grow in lawns. When they have been cut by the lawnmower a few times they learn to grow their flowers on shorter stems so that they won't be chopped off.

Follow-up activities

✧ Pick some long daisies, split their stems with your fingernail then thread them into each other to make a daisy chain.
✧ Make a daisy chain display (see Chapter 7).
✧ Dye some wild grass. Stand it in a jar of hot water, coloured with food dye.
✧ Use fluted pastry cutters on pieces of thin sliced bread to make flowers you can eat. Spread these shapes with different coloured jams or honey, and decorate the middle with a Smartie.
✧ Sing and play 'In and Out the Dusty Bluebells' from *Oranges and Lemons* compiled by Karen King [OUP].
✧ Say the action poem 'Daisy chain' on page 69 of the Resources section.

GARDEN TOOLS

Objective

Music – To find out how garden tools are used and to play and sing an action song to the tune of 'Here We Go Round the Mulberry Bush'.

Group size

Twelve children.

What you need

A garden spade, fork, rake and hoe, a pair of secateurs, a dibber or pencil, a watering can.

Discussion

Gardens are places to grow food and flowers and to relax. What can make gardening easier? A spade is used to dig the earth and turn it over in one lump. Why does it have a sharp edge? A fork has prongs and is also used to dig the soil and break up large lumps. Raking the soil smoothes out lumps and leaves it fine and crumbly, suitable for growing seeds. Pushing or pulling a hoe through the top layer of soil, when it is dry and crusty, will help break it up. A hoe is also used to uproot weeds. When bushes and flowers grow too tall, secateurs are used to cut them back. Do secateurs look like a tool the children use? Which tool would gather leaves off the lawn? A dibber is like a pencil and is used to make holes in the soil to plant seedlings. These seedlings should never be allowed to dry out and must be kept moist with the watering can. What other tools and equipment are used for gardening? How is the lawn cut? Remember gardening tools are sharp and can be dangerous.

What to do

Demonstrate the actions people make with the tools. Form a circle with the children holding hands and move round as you all sing the chorus of 'Here We Go Round the Mulberry Bush'. When you get to the end of the chorus, stop moving. The teacher then holds up the spade and the children sing 'This is how we dig with the spade' and make the appropriate action. Sing the chorus again, then mime as you sing 'This is the way we use the fork'. Repeat the process for each of the gardening tools.

Follow-up activities

✧ Take the group outside and show them how to use the tools in the earth.
✧ Make patterns in the surface of a polystyrene food tray using a hand trowel, hand fork and dibber.
✧ Push some dried garden soil through a garden sieve to make it fine enough for planting tiny seeds.
✧ To sow seeds in a straight row you need a garden line. Tie a two-metre length of cord between two chair legs and ask the children to walk in a straight line along it.
✧ Prepare a patch of earth and sow some pansy or marigold seeds.
✧ Sing the song 'Grandad loves his garden' on page 82 of the Resources section.

MY OWN GARDEN

Objectives

Design and Technology – To plan and make a mini-garden using a range of materials.

Group size

Six children.

What you need

Plastic or polystyrene food trays or vegetable punnets from the greengrocer at least 4cm deep, pencils, writing paper, scissors, a bucket of small washed pebbles (these are cheaper if bought unwashed from a builders' merchant), all-purpose compost, foil plates, grass seed, a packet of common thyme seeds, play people, toy garden swings and animals, a water container with a spray attachment.

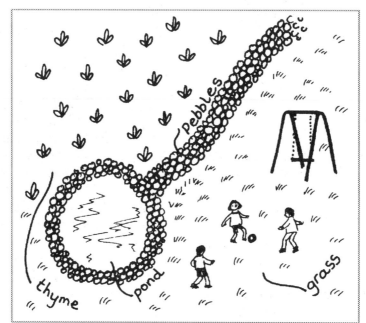

What to do

Tell the children they are going to make their own mini-garden and ask them to think of how they want to divide their garden and then to draw a plan of it on paper. They should put a layer of pebbles (for drainage) in the base of their container. Cover the pebbles with compost and press it down gently (with a flat hand) so that it comes to just under the rim. They can use the end of a pencil to mark out their planned areas in the compost then water it.

Cut and position some foil (from a foil plate) for a pond, if wanted. Lay down some pebbles for paths.

Sow the grass and thyme seeds in the appropriate areas and cover lightly with a thin layer of compost.

Put the mini-garden in a transparent polythene bag and leave it in a warm, light place. In about five days, when the smallest seedlings will have grown to a height of one centimetre, remove the plastic bag.

Arrange the garden toys, people and animals in position. Spray the garden with water frequently to keep it moist. Do not let it become too wet.

Discussion

Gardens are often divided up into areas for different purposes such as growing flowers and vegetables, lawn and play areas, a pond and paths. Some people don't have gardens but still want to grow something. They use window-boxes, hanging baskets or pots on a balcony. Why would they have to water plants in containers more often than plants which are growing in the garden? A few insects eat growing plants and are a pest. How can we encourage birds to come into the garden and eat the insects? A garden pond can be made using an old sink or half-barrel. Birds can land on a large stone in the pond, and have a bath. Frogs can leap out of the pond to catch slugs in the garden. Why should children's swings be positioned on the lawn?

Follow-up activities

✧ Use scissors to cut the grass in your mini-garden.
✧ Make an instant garden by 'planting' twigs, leaves and flowers into some damp earth in a shallow dish.
✧ Plant an 'animal barrel' for fun using some of the following plants: catmint, dogwood, horseradish, spider plants, cowslips, crab apple, pussy willow and bird cherry.
✧ Say the poem 'The swing' from *A Child's Garden of Verses* by Robert Louis Stevenson (Wordsworth).

CHAPTER 5
GROWING OUR FOOD

Fresh food is often processed before we buy it from the supermarket. This can make it difficult for children to recognise that it has been grown. In this chapter the children will be able to handle a variety of food and learn about the places where it has been grown.

PEELING FRUIT

Objective

Drama – To look at a variety of fruit and their peel and express the differences through mime.

Group size

The whole group.

What you need

An apple, pear, banana, orange, grapefruit, some grapes and cherries, a melon, a bowl of cold water, a knife, a large plate.

What to do

Let the children handle the pieces of fruit and show them how to peel the ones which need to be peeled before they can be eaten. Wash the rest of the fruit. Pull the citrus fruits into segments and point out the pips. Pull some of the grapes and cherries off their stalks and cut them open to display the stones. Wash the apple and pear, twist off the stalks then cut them in half to display the pips. Cut the melon in half. Put all the prepared fruit on a plate.

Ask the children to act out how they would peel and eat the fruit, remembering to get rid of the pips or stones. Suggest that some of them mime being a piece of fruit. A group could arrange themselves to represent the segments of an orange. Some of them can pretend to be a banana with one child standing upright in the middle and the others standing round him backwards and bending like a banana being peeled. Two friends can pretend to be two cherries and others can bunch together like grapes.

Discussion

Fruit grows on trees and bushes and its function is to hold and protect seeds. Although we can eat many different kinds of fruit there are some that would be harmful to eat. Why do we need to peel some pieces of fruit yet only wash others? Some fruit has only one seed inside while others have lots. Can the children give some examples?

Apples, pears, cherries and grapes grow in this country but are not ready to eat until autumn, after the summer sun has ripened them. Bananas, oranges, grapefruits and some melons will only grow in hot countries which have much more sun than we do.

Eating raw fruit is very good for people because it contains lots of vitamins to help us grow strong and healthy.

Follow-up activities

✧ Wear a blindfold and play a game of tasting fruit and guessing what it is.
✧ Make some clay fruit and paint it.
✧ Use a squeezer to make some fresh orange juice.
✧ Say the action rhyme 'The Cherry Tree' from *Round and Round the Garden* by Sarah Williams (OUP).
✧ Make a cut right at the end of a banana and see if you can see the letter 'y'.
✧ Sing 'Bananas in Pyjamas' from *Apusskidu: 56 Songs For Children* (A & C Black).

FUNNY PEAS

Objective

Geography – To help children understand that vegetables will only grow at certain times of year in this country.

Group size

Six children.

What you need

Fresh pea pods (frozen peas will do if fresh aren't available), a knife and fork, some coloured card (not green), a quarter of a packet of green crêpe paper, scissors, glue and spreaders.

Preparation

Draw the outline of a knife (approx. 16cm in length) on the card and cut out one outline for each child. Cut up the crêpe paper to make lots of squares (approx. 3 × 3cm).

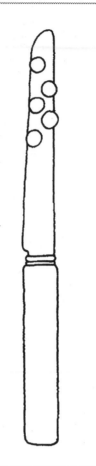

What to do

Let the children try to balance as many of the real peas as possible on the fork and then on the knife. Tell them this rhyme:

I eat my peas with honey, I've done so all my life.
It makes the peas taste funny, but it keeps them on my knife.

Give each child a little pile of the green squares and a card knife outline. Show them how to screw up each piece of crêpe paper into a little ball. When they have made enough crêpe peas to cover the blade of their card knife they can glue them on.

Discussion

What type of food are peas? Do the children know the names of other vegetables? In this country peas will only grow in the summer when the weather is really warm. What makes it possible for us to eat peas in the colder months of winter? (Peas can be frozen, dried or tinned.) Which other vegetables will grow only in the summer? Some vegetables, such as swedes, can be grown in the cold winter months because the main part of them grows under the soil where it is warmer. How do the children manage to eat their peas? Why do they think it would be dangerous to put a knife into their mouth? Does honey go well with peas? If not, what does?

Follow-up activities

✧ Sing the action rhyme 'Five Fat Peas' from *Round and Round the Garden* by Sarah Williams (OUP).

✧ Tell the story of 'The Princess and the Pea' from the *Kingfisher Treasury of Nursery Stories* by S. Price (Kingfisher).

✧ Draw a bed with lots of mattresses and a pea underneath the bottom one.

✧ Make a collection of vegetables which are different colours: orange (marrow, carrot), red (radish, cabbage), purple (beetroot, aubergine), yellow (pepper, corn), white (cauliflower, turnip), green (beans, broccoli), brown (potato, onion). Smell them all.

✧ Scrub potatoes, prick them with a fork and bake them in a hot oven for about one hour. Split them open, add some butter, watch it melt then eat them!

✧ Compare tinned peas, dried peas and frozen peas. Which kind of pea do the children like best?

CRISPY COLESLAW

Objective

Design and Technology – To cut vegetables using different tools and produce a salad to eat.

Group size

Six children.

What you need

White cabbage, six medium-sized carrots, salad cream, a potato peeler, a grater, a chopping board and knife, six pairs of scissors (to cut up the cabbage), a mixing bowl, a dessertspoon and fork, six plastic containers with lids (such as cottage cheese cartons).

What to do

Before the food is prepared the children will need to wash their hands.

Show them how they can use the potato peeler to peel the carrots, and supervise them closely when they cut the ends off with the knife. Peel the outer leaves from the cabbage, discard them and the children can then pull off two leaves each. Let them decide how to prepare each vegetable – either to cut them with the scissors or shred them using the grater. Put all the prepared vegetables together into the mixing bowl. Add salad cream and stir it into the vegetables. The children can then spoon some of the salad into their own container to take home with them.

Discussion

Coleslaw is a type of salad made with raw vegetables. What other vegetables can be eaten raw? Why was it easier to grate the carrot and cut the cabbage? The part of the carrot we eat is the root which grows below ground. Why was it necessary to peel it first? Wild creatures like to eat vegetables when they are growing. Who can guess why cabbage leaves sometimes have holes in them? Can the children think of ways to stop rabbits and birds destroying vegetables as they sprout from the ground?

If you want to keep your teeth healthy, is it better to eat raw vegetables or sweets?

Follow-up activities

✧ Cut a hard white cabbage down the middle. Look at how the leaves grow out from the stalk and how they all fit into each other. Peel the leaves off one half and compare the bulk to that of the other half.

✧ Cut 2cm off the top of a carrot and place it flat-side down in a dish of water. After a few days the top of the carrot will start to grow green shoots.

✧ Make a collection of vegetables and sort them according to those which grow above the ground and those which grow below.

✧ Make a chart using pictures of different-shaped vegetables. Label the columns: 'long ones', 'big round ones', 'small round ones', 'other shapes' and place the pictures in the correct column.

✧ Sing 'The cabbage patch' from *Up, Up and Away* by Derek Pearson (OUP).

✧ Say the action rhyme 'Old Tom tomato' from *This Little Puffin* compiled by Elizabeth Matterson (Puffin).

SNAP, CRACKLE AND POP

Objective

Music — To listen to a story about growing crops and make percussion sounds to accompany the story events.

Group size

The whole group.

What you need

Two sheets of coarse sandpaper, a bicycle security padlock and chain, a wooden spoon, a comb, bubble wrap, a ping-pong ball, a plastic bottle half full of pebbles, an empty food tub, a large paintbrush, a sheet of foil, brown paper and greaseproof paper.

What to do

Tell the children that they are going to take it in turns to make percussion sounds to accompany a story about cornfields. It might go like this: Mr Farmer decides that it's time to sow the corn. He starts up his tractor (*rub sheets of sandpaper together*) which pulls the plough through the hard earth. Then the harrow (*clank bicycle padlock and chain*) rakes it smooth. The seed drill machine (*say shh shh*) pushes the seeds into the soil. The crows (*say caw caw*) and the corncrakes (*grate wooden spoon across comb*) crack open some of the seeds (*burst bubble wrap*). The mice scratch in the earth for seeds (*fingernails scratch ping-pong ball*). As the shoots start to grow, more wildlife appears.

The rabbits and hares thud across the ground (*beat hands on chest*) to find young green shoots to munch. Hedgehogs dig for worms (*slide finger across flat foil*). Insects buzz (*children buzz*) in and out of the wild flowers looking for nectar. All the creatures are very busy looking for food and hiding from other animals who might eat them. The rain falls (*beat fingertips on an upturned food tub*) and waters the crops which grow tall in the bright warm sun. The corn sways and sighs in the breeze (*move soft paintbrush across brown paper*) and soon it's time for Mr Farmer to gather it in. Once the animals hear the sound of the combine harvester (*clank chains and rub sandpaper*) coming to collect the grain they rush away (*pound chest*) and hide in the branches of the hedgerows (*rustle greaseproof paper*).

Discussion

Farmers grow cereal plants — oats, wheat, rye, maize, barley and rice. Which cereals do the children eat for breakfast? These cereal crops grow as tall as long grass and their seeds are called corn.

Follow-up activities

✧ Make a display of patchwork cornfields (see Chapter 7).
✧ Open a tin of sweetcorn and compare the corn with the seeds on a corn cob (maize).
✧ Blend one dessertspoon of cornflour (ground maize) with two spoonfuls of cold water. Heat it with four more spoonfuls of water and watch it thicken like custard.
✧ Sing and play 'The Farmer's in his Den' from *Oranges and Lemons* compiled by Karen King (OUP).
✧ Say the poem 'The farmer knows' on page 72 of the Resources section.

DINGLE, DANGLE SCARECROW

❋ ❋

Objective

Mathematics – To make a scarecrow picture using different shapes.

Group size

Six children.

What you need

For each child: a gummed circle, a gummed rectangle, a wooden lolly stick, a twig about 18cm in length, felt to use for the hat, A4 paper to serve as a background, straw (a bag of meadow hay from a pet shop), adhesive tape, glue and spreaders, felt-tipped pens.

Preparation

Cut out six gummed circles with a diameter of 5cm and six gummed rectangles 5cm × 10cm. Cut the felt into a T-shape to use as the scarecrow's hat.

What to do

Explain to the children that they are going to make a scarecrow picture. Ensure that they know the names of the shapes they are going to use. Help them to tape the twig in place across the middle of the paper for the scarecrow's arms and to glue the lolly stick about 4cm below these arms. They can stick the oblong 'body' over the top of the tape and the stick (as shown in the illustration). Ask the children to stick the circle on to the body and to glue some straw on the top of his head before they glue the hat on at a jaunty angle. Let them draw in the face – it may look fierce!

Discussion

Farmers have to protect their growing crops from pests that like to eat them. Which creatures are pests to the farmer? Why would a scarecrow scare birds away? What food do farmers grow for us to eat? There are many different types of farms. Some grow cereals, or fruit, or vegetables. There are farms which only have pigs or sheep or hens, while others grow animal food such as barley, oats, sugar

beet and grass. Sometimes grass is left to grow very long before it is cut. After it has been cut it is left lying on the ground in the sun. When it has dried out it is ready to be tied up into bales of hay for cows, horses and sheep to eat. Hens eat corn and then lay eggs in straw nests. Straw comes from the stalks of the corn crops after the grain (seeds) has been removed.

Follow-up activities

✧ Introduce other geometric shapes such as triangles and squares. Ask the children to look round the room to find examples of triangles, squares, rectangles and circles.
✧ Use art straws to make geometric shapes then count how many sides each shape has.
✧ Sing and play 'The Scarecrow' from *Oranges and Lemons* compiled by Karen King (OUP).
✧ Make a collection of different types of corn (including barley, oats, rice and wheat).
✧ Bake some flapjacks using porridge oats.
✧ Look at pictures of old farming methods using a horse and plough. Compare them to modern methods using tractors and combine harvesters. Which do the children think are better?
✧ Sing the song 'Dingle, dangle scarecrow' on page 84 of the Resources section.

HARVEST TIME

Objective

Religious Education – To be involved in thanksgiving for food which has been grown for us.

Group size

Six children.

What you need

One copy of the photocopiable sheet on page 94 made on thin card for each child, 36 counters or buttons to use for covering the apples in the bowls, scissors, a set of cards showing the letters of the alphabet, an empty food carton to put the letter cards in.

Preparation

Cut up the sheet on page 94 to make six apple bowl cards. Make a set of individual alphabet letters on cards, mix them up and put them in the carton.

What to do

Play 'Apple Bingo'. Let the children take it in turns to read out the letters which are printed on their apple bowl card. Give each child six counters and explain to them that you are going to take out one letter card at a time from the carton and show it to them. (If they can't identify the letter then tell them its name.) If they have the same letter on one of the apples in their bowl, they should cover it with a counter. When they have covered all the apples on their card they can call out 'Bingo'. The children can then play the game again using a different bowl card.

Discussion

When a farmer's crops have grown ripe and are ready for eating, they need to be gathered in or harvested. There are machines which collect grain, dig up potatoes and other vegetables and shake fruit off trees into a net underneath. Can the children guess which fruit and vegetables need to be hand picked? In bad weather, crops cannot grow and the harvest may be poor. A good harvest means that there will be plenty of food and everyone can then join in thanksgiving. People celebrate the harvest in different ways. Christians decorate their churches with fruit, flowers, vegetables and loaves of bread (made with flour from ground corn). Jewish people build a little shelter which has fruit and vegetables hanging from the roof. For a week they eat all their meals in this shelter called a *Sukkah*. Hindus sing, dance and feast to celebrate their harvest festival called *Vaisaki*. Buddhists have a 'first fruit' ceremony when they offer Buddha a large bowl of milk and rice.

Follow-up activities

✧ Make apple boats by cutting an apple into eighths and then spreading each with a little honey before eating.
✧ Design and make a harvesting machine using construction equipment. What is the machine called?
✧ Arrange a harvest display in your room. You can include harvest fruits for animals, such as acorns, beech nuts and flower seed heads.
✧ Say the action rhyme 'The Apple Tree' from *Round and Round the Garden* by Sarah Williams (OUP).
✧ Act out the poem 'The crop song' on page 70 of the Resources section.
✧ Read the poem 'Haytime' from *The Book of a Thousand Poems* (Collins).

MAGIC BALLOON

Objective

Science – To watch a balloon being blown up by yeast, which is a living plant.

Group size

Six children.

What you need

Three flat teaspoonfuls of dried, granular, active baking yeast or two 7g packets (don't use easy-blend yeast), three flat teaspoonfuls of sugar, 100ml of warm water (blood heat), a funnel, an empty one litre clear plastic bottle, a balloon.

What to do

Inspect and smell the yeast and tip it through the funnel into the bottle. Add the sugar and water, and shake the mixture gently. Fix the balloon around the neck of the bottle (as shown in the illustration), and leave it in a warm room where it can be seen. After 15 minutes the balloon should have started to inflate, and after two hours it should be as big as an adult's head. Leave it all day to see what happens.

Discussion

Yeast is a living plant that does not have flowers or seeds. To make new plants it grows tiny little buds. Yeast will start to grow in a mixture of sugar and warm water. While it is feeding on the sugar it is growing. You can see it bubbling as it gives off a gas (carbon dioxide), rather like when people breathe. We can blow up a balloon using our breath and the yeast can blow up a balloon using the gas it produces. Bread is made using flour (crushed corn grains) and other ingredients. Can the children guess what it is that makes the air bubbles in bread?

If bread is made without yeast it does not have any air bubbles and is very hard to eat. Yeast plants are very important because some are used in the making of medicine and others in the making of cheese, beer and wine. Yeasts also help leaves to change into compost to make food for green plants.

Follow-up activities

✧ Buy some fresh yeast from a baker's. Smell it, feel it and look at it through a magnifying glass (don't let the children eat it).
✧ Make up two bread mixtures (one with yeast, the other without). Compare their sizes after leaving them both covered in a warm place for an hour. Bake the one that has risen.
✧ Blow some bubbles into the air using soapy water. What do they have inside them?
✧ Make a bubble picture. Blow down a straw into a bowl of soapy, coloured water until the bubbles rise up above the rim. Gently place some paper over the top and press down. Lift the paper away and see a bubble pattern.
✧ Say the poem 'The King's Breakfast' from *When We Were Very Young* by A. A. Milne (Mammoth).
✧ Say the poem 'The balloon' on page 74 of the Resources section.
✧ Sing 'Red balloons' from *Count Me In* (A & C Black).

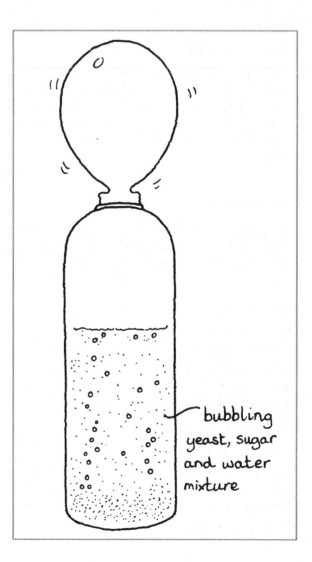

bubbling yeast, sugar and water mixture

SUPERMARKETS

● ●

Objective

Geography – To show children that we eat food which is grown in different parts of the world.

Group size

Eight children.

What you need

Empty food packets, boxes, yoghurt and other cartons, plastic drink bottles, drink cans, fruit nets and rubber bands, construction toys such as LEGO, building bricks (to use as blocks of cheese or butter), a torch to use as a bar-code scanner, a toy till or box with plastic money (milkbottle tops, counters or tiddly-winks), thick card, scales, plastic carrier bags, three or four garden hanging baskets, two freezer baskets, two dolls' prams, rope or thick string.

Preparation

Fill the fruit nets with pieces of construction toys to serve as pretend fruit and vegetables, secure the tops with rubber bands. Cut up some pieces of thick card to about the size of a credit card. Remove the chains from the hanging baskets and make handles of rope (old skipping rope) or thick string so that they can be carried like shopping baskets. Tie the freezer baskets in place on top of the dolls' prams to make shopping trolleys.

What to do

Talk about the food and drink that was in the containers, and check the labels for the countries where they were grown.

Ask the children to help move the tables into position to make the aisles of the supermarket and lay out the goods on the tables. Set up a chair and table for the checkout and arrange the scales, scanner, till, money, credit cards and carrier bags ready for use. Let the children play at shopping in a supermarket. They can take it in turns to be a customer, a checkout assistant, a shelf filler or a manager.

Discussion

Do the children realise that some foods are grown abroad? Bananas grow in bunches (like fingers on a hand pointing upwards) in countries which have plenty of water and heat. Why do oranges and lemons grow on trees in Israel and Spain and not in this country? Sugar is produced from boiling sugar cane which is a type of very tall grass. The cane grows well in India and Cuba which are hot, wet countries. Rice likes hot and steamy weather and begins growing under mud in the paddy fields of countries like India and China. Paddy is the name given to the growing grains of rice.

Follow-up activities

✧ Draw an item of foreign food and find the country where it was grown on a world map . Fix your drawing to this position on the map.

✧ Cut out pictures of food from magazines and stick them on to the outline of a supermarket trolley (see illustration below).

✧ Talk about what shopping was like before there were supermarkets.

✧ Say the poem 'At the supermarket' from *Up, Up and Away* by Derek Pearson (OUP).

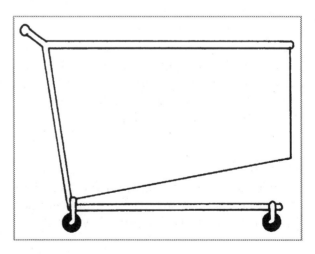

CHAPTER SIX
USING THINGS THAT GROW

Nowadays many goods are manufactured from synthetic materials. Before technology was so advanced people had to rely on plants to provide them with the raw materials for making things. This chapter shows some of the ways in which plants can be used in our everyday lives.

LAVENDER'S BLUE

Objective

History — To find out how and why herbs were used in the past and to make a sachet of lavender.

Group size

Six children.

What you need

A J-cloth, a ruler, a pencil, scissors, 25g dried lavender flower heads, a tablespoon, 12 rubber bands, 3 metres of ribbon or thick wool.

Preparation

Use the pencil and ruler to mark out the J-cloth into squares (approx. 18cm × 18cm).

What to do

Help each of the children to cut out a square of J-cloth. Let them handle and smell the lavender and put one teaspoon of it into the middle of their J-cloth square. Carefully gather the corners up to form a pouch and secure it with two rubber bands. Show the children how to measure half a metre of ribbon, cut it and help them to tie it into a bow round the neck of the bag.

Discussion

Lavender is an evergreen plant known as a herb. It has blue or mauve flowers and a very sweet smell which bees and butterflies love. When the flower heads are dried they can be used to fill a sachet and be put in a drawer, hidden among clothes to make them smell nice. Ask the children where they will keep their lavender sachet.

There are many kinds of herbs which people through the ages have grown for different reasons. Mint is a herb which is often used to flavour food. What do the children eat which is mint flavoured? (Chocolates, spearmint sweets, toothpaste.) Herbs were also used as medicine and even today people take garlic pills to keep them staying healthy. Dentists use cloves in some mixtures they make for fillings. Herbs can be crushed to squeeze out their oil which is then used to perfume make-up, scent and soap. You can wash your hair with rosemary shampoo and wash your hands with lemon verbena soap. Some herbs are grown because they look so pretty. Why is a herb garden a wonderful place for a blind person to visit?

Basil

Marjoram

Mint

Rosemary

Lavender

Follow-up activities

✧ Try making another sachet, this time using dried rosemary or thyme.

✧ Sing the nursery rhyme 'Lavender's Blue Dilly Dilly' from *The Kingfisher Nursery Collection* (Kingfisher).

✧ Use herbs and other strong-smelling substances such as coffee, Marmite, pickle, soap and washing-up liquid to play a smelling game. Can the children identify the substances by smell if blindfolded?

✧ Make some peppermint creams to eat.

✧ Mix dried herbs, dried flower petals and lemon or orange peel. Put this pot-pourri into a pot with a tight-fitting lid. When you want to freshen your room and make it smell sweet, open the pot and shake gently.

THREE LITTLE PIGS

Objective

Design and Technology – To design and make houses which the Three Little Pigs might have built using a range of materials.

Group size

Six children.

What you need

A copy of the story 'The Three Little Pigs', straw (a bag of meadow hay from a pet shop will do), twigs or sticks (halved canes from a garden centre), Plasticine, plastic or wooden construction bricks.

What to do

Read or tell the children the story of 'The Three Little Pigs'. Show them the materials you have provided and plan with them how they could make houses like those of the little pigs. Let the children work in pairs and allow each pair a chance to use the straw, sticks and bricks to build their model houses. If they run into difficulties you could suggest that they hollow out the straw like a nest. If the sticks will not stay up recommend that one stick is pushed into a Plasticine 'mat' to serve as a central pole and the other sticks can meet it at the top to make a cone shape. To make the brick house sturdy, the children will need to build with the bricks in a staggered fashion. When they have

finished, they should test the strength of their buildings by blowing, pushing or knocking them.

Discussion

Which of the buildings was the strongest? The first type of houses that people built were made of mud, grass, bark and twigs. These weren't strong enough to cope with bad weather so people started using bricks to build their homes. These bricks were also made of materials which were grown. Clay was mixed with straw or grass and then left to dry in the sun. Nowadays, bricks are made without straw but there are still houses which use reeds or straw to thatch their roofs. In Asia, some houses are built of bamboo which is a giant woody grass plant. What else can bamboo be used for? In parts of Africa, people live in huts which are made from woven grasses. How are baskets made?

Follow-up activities

✧ There are many different types of homes. What kind of house do the children live in?
✧ Think of all the things that would be needed to build a house: wood, nails, floorboards, roof tiles, windows.
✧ Use Constructo-straws to make the framework for different-shaped houses.
✧ What are the names of the homes of pigs, horses, birds, mice (and other animals)?
✧ Read the poem 'House Coming Down' by Eleanor Farjeon from *The Young Puffin Book of Verse* compiled by Barbara Ireson.
✧ Draw patterns on a semicircle of paper then, twist it round and fasten it to make a cone shape that looks like a North American Indian's wigwam.
✧ Sing the song 'The three little pigs' on page 86 of the Resources section.
✧ Say the rhyme 'A hive for a honey bee' from *This Little Puffin* compiled by Elizabeth Matterson (Puffin).
✧ Say the poem 'The shiny little house' from *The Book of a Thousand Poems* (Collins).

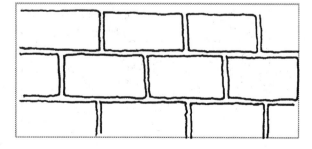

RINGS AND BALLS

Objective

Physical Education — To have fun playing with rings and balls made of rubber from a rubber tree.

Group size

The whole group.

What you need

An assortment of large, medium and small rubber balls including tennis balls, six rubber quoits, six empty plastic drink bottles, three plastic drink bottles filled with gravel or sand with their lids screwed on tightly, an empty bucket and a house brick, a rubber safety mat.

Preparation

Set up the circuit of small games equipment as shown in Figure 1.

What to do

Explain to the children that they are all going to take turns to stop and play at each 'station' of the circuit. Show them how they should use each piece of equipment. At Station 1, they will throw the hoops over the bottles; at 2, they will bounce the big balls with the flat of their hand; at 3, they will kneel about two metres away from a partner and roll the ball straight across the floor to each other; at 4, they will knock over as many bottles as they can with one strong roll of the ball; at 5, they will throw the balls into the bucket that is leaning on the brick; at 6, they will do a somersault on the mat. This last activity will need the most supervision to make sure that heads are tucked well in before pushing off with feet. Warn the children of the dangers of throwing balls too high or too hard.

Discussion

Balls, quoits and safety mats are bouncy and are made of rubber. What else is made of rubber? (Rubbers, balloons.) When a hole is made in the bark of a rubber tree a milk-like liquid flows out. It is this sticky gum which is used to make rubber. Rubber stretches and is used in elastic to keep up socks and trousers and to make rubber bands. It can be pushed into the top of bottles to be used as stoppers and is also used for bouncy castles. Rubber is waterproof and is used to make raincoats. Which other waterproof things are made of rubber? (Rubber gloves, boats, flippers.) Bicycle tyres and car tyres need to be strong, flexible and waterproof — they are also made of rubber.

Follow-up activities

✧ Use the photocopiable sheet on page 95 and draw lines to match ball to bucket, shuttlecock to bat, ring to stand and child to hoop. How many are left over in each picture?
✧ Nip the top leaf off a rubber plant and watch the gum flow.
✧ Test different fabrics to see if they are waterproof (include rubber gloves and wellingtons).
✧ Cut an old tennis ball in half to see what it is made of.
✧ Say the rhyme 'Each India rubber ball' from *Up, Up and Away* by Derek Pearson (OUP).
✧ Say the poem 'Happiness' from *When We Were Very Young* by A. A. Milne (Methuen).

EASTER CHICK

* *

Objective

Design and Technology – To feel the softness of wool and to make an Easter chick.

Group size

Six children.

What you need

100g of yellow double-knit economy wool, a full-sized straight-backed chair, scraps of yellow and black felt or card, scissors with long blades, a glue stick.

Preparation

To prepare separate balls of wool for each child, wind wool from the main ball round the back of the chair about 16 times, cut it off and then roll it up. Make six balls in this way then cut six 20cm lengths of wool. For the beak cut out a joined double triangle (or diamond) of yellow felt and cut two round black felt eyes for each chick.

What to do

Show the children how to wind their ball of wool round their four spread fingers to make loops (see illustration). Slide the loops off their fingers and tie them together tightly in the middle with the 20cm length of wool. Carefully cut the loops at each end and you will have the fluffy body of a chick. Add glue to the double beak and the black eyes and stick them on to the chick.

Discussion

When a chick hatches out of an egg its feathers are damp and straggly but soon dry to look like a yellow fluffy ball. The soft woolly hair of a sheep's coat feels fluffy and is called the fleece. Sheep grow their coats to keep warm in winter while they are eating grass on the hillsides. Why do we cut off (shear) their woolly coats at the beginning of the summer? This does not hurt the sheep at all; it's like when people have their hair cut. If we don't shear the sheep their coats fall off naturally in stages but this takes a long time. After the fleece is cut, it is combed to remove tangles and plant seeds which may have become caught in it. When the wool has been spun on a spinning wheel into one long piece called yarn, it is ready to knit or weave into various things. What warm things can the children think of that are made of wool? (Socks, overcoats, carpets, blankets ...) Wool is also gathered from some types of goats, rabbits and camels.

Follow-up activities

✧ Make a nest for the chick. Glue the inside of an empty mousse carton and line it with rabbit bedding straw from a pet shop.
✧ Loosen the strands of a piece of wool and look at them through a magnifying glass.
✧ Cut 8cm lengths of different-coloured wools. Mix them all together and then let the children sort them into colours.
✧ Sing 'Baa Baa Black Sheep' and 'Mary Had a Little Lamb'.
✧ Make a 'feely' bag using different materials including wool. Ask the children to guess which fabric they are feeling.
✧ Say the rhyme 'Help me wind my ball of wool' from *Up, Up and Away* by Derek Pearson (OUP).
✧ Say the poem 'Five fluffy chicks' from *This Little Puffin* compiled by Elizabeth Matterson (Puffin).

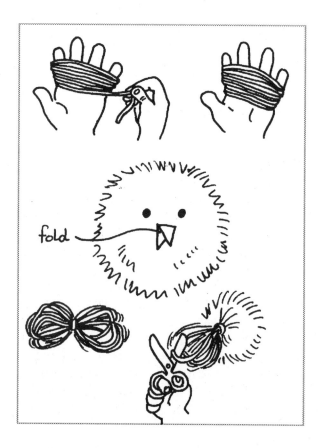

MASHED PAPER

Objective

Geography – To help preserve the environment by using recycled paper to make a paper orange.

Group size

Six children.

What you need

Ten large sheets of newspaper (20 of tabloid size), a plastic washing-up bowl, a litre of water, 50g of flour, a dinner plate, a pot of mixed orange paint and brushes, PVA adhesive for glaze.

What to do

Tear the sheets of newspaper up into small pieces about the size of a child's hand. Put them into the bowl and pour the water over them. Make sure that all the paper is wet. Leave it to stand for a couple of hours until most of the water has been absorbed. Pour off any excess water and sprinkle on the flour. Let the children stand around the bowl and squeeze and knead the mixture with their hands until it is thoroughly mashed. They can then take a handful of the pulp each and, with two hands, form it into a ball about the size of a tangerine. Leave the balls on the plate for about five days until they have dried out completely. Paint them orange and when dry glaze them with diluted PVA adhesive which will be transparent when dry.

Discussion

Most paper is made from trees. Once the tree has been cut down its wood is broken up into very small pieces and mixed to a pulp with water. It is spread out flat and pressed till all the water is squeezed out and then left to dry. Ask the children to suggest ways in which paper is used (to make wallpaper, wrapping paper, writing paper, money, stamps, books, comics, plates). Because we use paper for so many things we cut down far too many trees. Why do we need to save as many growing trees as possible? Trees are very important as homes for wildlife, to stop soil being washed away by the rain, to provide us and animals with shade from the burning sun, to grow leaves which

some folded newspapers

a lump of papier-mâché on a board

a bowl of gleaming (painted) papier-mâché oranges

fall and become compost. How can paper be saved? If newspapers are taken to paper banks they can be recycled which means fewer trees will need to be cut down.

Follow-up activities

✧ Make some other kinds of fruit using more mashed paper.

✧ Play a game of musical islands. Each child stands on a piece of newspaper. When the music starts they dance around but when it stops they must rush back to their island.

✧ Make a collection of different kinds of paper. How many kinds can be found?

✧ Pick up any litter in your room, put it in the wastepaper bin and keep the environment clean.

✧ Say the poem 'If all the world was paper' from *The Oxford Nursery Rhyme Book* compiled by Iona and Peter Opie.

✧ Say the poem 'Newspapers' from *Seeing and Doing Anthology* (Thames Television, OP).

BOBBING BOATS

Objective

Science – To make a catamaran sailing boat which will float because air trapped in cork makes it lighter than water.

Group size

Six children.

What you need

12 bottle corks, 12 wooden cocktail sticks, six rubber bands, white paper for the sails, scissors, pencils, rulers, crayons or felt-tipped pens, adhesive tape, a washing-up bowl half-full of water.

Preparation

Cut six pieces of paper measuring 8cm × 3cm for the sails. (Some children may be able to do this for themselves.)

What to do

Help the children to secure two corks side-by-side with a rubber band and to push a cocktail stick carefully into each cork (see illustration below). They can choose a pattern to decorate one side or both sides of their sail with the felt-tipped pens and then fix this sail to the top of both cocktail sticks with the adhesive tape. Let the children test to see if their boat will float in the bowl of water.

Discussion

Do the children know what the outside skin of a tree is called? Cork is the bark of an evergreen oak tree. Every ten years or so the bark is stripped off the tree, but it does not harm it. Look carefully at the little splits and holes in a cork which are the pores (openings) through which the tree bark used to breathe. Cork does not let water in and can be squashed to go into the top of a wine bottle. As the cork springs back into shape it pushes against the sides of the bottle and stops air from getting in and wine from spilling out. It is the air trapped in the cork which makes it light enough to float on water. Why are lifebelts on boats made of cork? Because cork stops heat or cold travelling through, it is very good for making table mats. Bathroom floor tiles are sometimes made of cork. Can the children guess why?

Follow-up activities

✧ Make a boat with only one cork and one sail and try floating it on water. What happens?
✧ Press corks into sponges dampened with different-coloured paints and then print a pattern on paper with them.
✧ Weigh two cork table mats separately. Place one in a bowl of water and see it float. After two hours weigh this wet one again and compare it to the weight of the dry one. You will find the floating cork has absorbed some water. Weigh it again after another two hours. Does the cork absorb enough water to make it sink?
✧ Say the poem 'A Sea Song from the Shore' from *The Book of a Thousand Poems* (Collins).
✧ Sing 'Bobby Shafto' from *Sing Hey diddle diddle* (A & C Black).
✧ Sing 'The big ship sails on the Alley, Alley O' from *Oranges and Lemons*, compiled by Karen King (OUP).

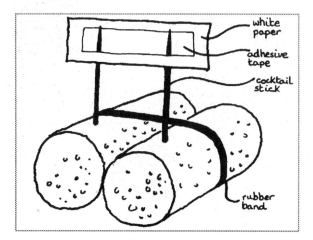

white paper
adhesive tape
cocktail stick
rubber band

T-SHIRTS

Objective

Mathematics – To fit 'T shapes' into each other and create an interesting pattern with cotton pieces.

Group size

Six children.

What you need

Cardboard, a ruler, six pencils, scissors, assorted pieces of thin cotton material, sharp fabric scissors, three pots of glue and six spreaders, six pieces of thick background paper (A4 size).

Preparation

Draw a 'T shape' on the card using the dimensions shown in Figure 1. Use this T-shirt template to cut out several layers of differently-patterned cotton material. The maximum number of T-shirts that can be fitted on to one background sheet is 16 so do not cut out more than 96 T-shirts! Of course, you can use far less to make an effective pattern.

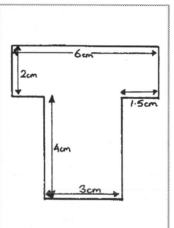

What to do

Tell the children how many T-shirt shapes they will each need for their pattern and let them count them out for themselves. Ask them to use the pieces to make a pattern on their background paper. Look to see if any of them have managed to fit them into each other (as shown in the illustration) and show the ones who haven't how to do so. If they are happy with their arrangement they can stick the T-shirts into place. When they have finished they can find each rectangle between the T-shirts and write a big T in this space with a pencil.

Discussion

Is anyone in the group wearing a T-shirt today? Why is it called a T-shirt? The shapes used for the pattern are made of cotton which comes from a growing plant. Cotton seeds are sown in fields and can grow into plants as tall as one metre. When the pods, called bolls, are ripe they burst open and show the seeds which are held within a mass of soft white fibres. The cotton field looks as if it is covered with lots of fluffy snowballs the size of apples. The cotton seeds are picked and separated from the white fluff. A machine spins the fluff into cotton thread and another machine weaves it into cloth for making clothes. What are cotton reels used for? How many things can children think of that are made of cotton?

Follow-up activities

✧ Tie-dye squares of white cotton fabric.
✧ Children can pencil their initials on a card and punch holes (not too close together) along the line of the letters. Use thick cotton thread to stitch along the outline.
✧ See how many cotton reels the children can build into a tower before the tower falls over.
✧ Examine a piece of cotton wool and pull it apart.
✧ Sing the action rhyme 'Wind the bobbin up' from *The Little Puffin* compiled by Elizabeth Matterson (Puffin).
✧ Make a collage using things that grow (see Chapter 7).

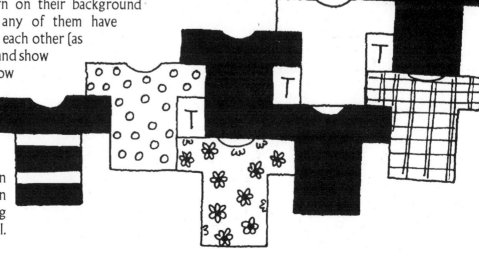

STRING STRANDS

. . . .

Objective

History – To look at how rope has been made in the past and to make a string tree picture.

Group size

Six children.

What you need

Six pieces of thick paper or card (about A4 size), thick garden twine which can be bought from a garden centre (synthetic string will not do), scissors, adhesive and spreaders.

What to do

Let the children look at the ball of string and help them to cut off a piece which is slightly shorter than the length of their piece of paper. Explain that they are going to use it to make the shape of a tree in winter. Show them how they can unravel the fibres of the string into strands but only undo just under half way. Each strand can then be teased out with fingernails until it is quite fluffy. Stick the 'trunk' part of the string on to the paper. Then spread out each unravelled strand before sticking it down in branch fashion as shown in the illustration. Don't stick down all the fluffy bits, they will look more realistic if left sticking up. Leave the tree pictures flat until the glue is dry.

Discussion

String is thin rope. Many thousands of years ago rope was made by plaiting grasses together. What other things have the children seen that are plaited? Nowadays, hemp, sisal and Manila plants are grown specially for making rope. Parts of the plants are twisted to make long pieces. A few of these pieces are then twisted together into thicker strands. The more strands there are in a piece of rope the stronger it is. How many strands were there in the string that the children pulled apart? Coir comes from the outside of coconuts and is used to make springy ropes which can float. Tugboats use tow-ropes made out of coir to pull other ships. Can the children think of how many uses there are for rope or string? (Washing line, rope ladder, yo-yo, guy ropes for a tent, pulling a sledge.)

Follow-up activities

✧ Practise tying knots in a piece of string and then try tying shoelaces.
✧ Tie three strands of string to the back of a chair and plait them.
✧ Ask two children to hold a skipping rope at each end and lay it across the ground for the others to jump over. Wriggle the rope from side to side or up and down (but still on the ground) to make it more difficult to jump over. Can any of the children slide under the rope if it is held 30cm off the ground?
✧ Dip a piece of string into thick paint then wiggle it over a piece of paper to make a pattern.
✧ Say the poem 'Wind on the hill' from *Now We Are Six* by A. A. Milne (Methuen).
✧ Sing 'Turn the rope' from *Knock at the Door* by Jan Betts (Ward Lock).

CHAPTER 7
DISPLAYS

Advertisement hoardings tell us about the latest products. Children's displays have the same function. Visitors will be able to see immediately what your children are learning and be able to judge how much you have encouraged them to be independent. Displays are your shop window, and as such need careful planning and structuring.

Displays not only reassure children how much we value their work but also demonstrate to parents and visitors what they are capable of producing. Parents are much more interested in seeing their own child's original art work and writing, however immature, than in seeing a neat and perfect display of what is obviously an adult's work. However, even though you are using very young children's work there are several ways this can be enhanced.

✧ First of all your displays need careful **planning**. Choose the title for your display, according to the season and to what is topical in the group. Don't be over ambitious and involve too many different processes. Ask the children for their ideas — these can be surprisingly innovative. Consider where you will put your display and at what height it will be positioned, bearing in mind whether you want the children to be able to touch it and read it for themselves.

✧ Try to make the display **three-dimensional**. Possible ways in which this can be achieved include: sticking bits of polystyrene or card behind a drawing to 'raise' it from the surface on which it is mounted; dangling work from the top of the display; limiting the stapling so that not everything is completely flat, i.e., leaving bits sticking up or out. If you can use a mixture of mediums such as paper, fabric and natural materials (e.g. grass or twigs) this will make the display more lively and varied.

✧ **Mounting** children's work on to backing paper will show it off like a picture in a frame. If you double mount their work (see illustration), it will add to the effect. A paper cutter or guillotine is invaluable for preparing the mounting paper.

✧ When you are ready to assemble the work, before you **staple** it into a fixed position, arrange it on the background using dressmaking or drawing pins. If you don't have a staple gun, an ordinary stapler can be opened up and pressed directly against the wall. If staples are difficult to remove you can buy a staple-remover from a stationer's.

✧ Ensure that your display has appropriate **labels**. Visitors will want to know what all those squiggles are supposed to be! The secret of good label writing is to draw faint pencil guidelines first and also to use the right pen. If you use a thick, dark, chisel-tip marker, your labels will stand out clearly.

✧ **Use** your displays. Read through them with the children and let them touch them if it's practical to do so. Don't be in a rush to replace displays, after all they do take a lot of valuable time to produce. You can always add to them or change parts of them as the project develops.

Finally, don't be too worried about scale and perspective, at this stage it's learning not the precision that counts.

POND LIFE

What you need

Black, brown and green tissue and / or crêpe paper, white card, scraps of lace or a doily, scissors, crayons or felt-tipped pens, thick black felt-tipped pens, bubble wrap, a black bin-bag, adhesive and spreaders, a large piece of blue backing paper to fit your display area, a staple gun, staples.

there is no room for the other wildlife. Some plants may need to be removed each year. There is such a lot to see, even in a small pond, but it is dangerous for young children to go to watch it on their own.

DAISY CHAIN

What you need

A large piece of pale green backing paper to fit your display area, a staple gun, sheets of white paper, sheets of green activity paper, a coffee mug, a penny, yellow and pink crayons, scissors, a craft knife, adhesive tape, pencils.

What to do

Staple the blue background paper to the display area. Make the water plants by tearing narrow strips of green tissue-paper. Give the children these strips and show them how to hold one end and twist the other end before fixing these spirals upright on to the background. Make other water weeds by cutting slits along the top edge of a rectangle of green crêpe paper to make a long fringe. Pleat this rectangle, gather it at the bottom and fix the bottom point to the background. It should fan out slightly. The children can screw up some brown tissue-paper to serve as underwater rocks and stones. Staple these weeds and stones on to the background. Draw a frog, a newt and a dragonfly on the white card (or maybe the children could do this), cut them out and let the children colour them and stick lace wings on to the dragonfly. Fix these and some bubble wrap frog-spawn (see the activity on page 22) among the weeds and stones. Cut out small circles of black plastic from the bin-bag to make water beetles. Stick these on to the 'pond' and let the children draw the black legs directly on to the background paper. They may need to stand on a stool to do this and can draw in some tadpoles at the same time.

Discussion

Ponds provide a habitat for a variety of wildlife. What do pond creatures eat? Water plants can grow so much that they nearly choke the pond and

What to do

Draw round the edge of the coffee mug on to the white paper and cut out one circle for each child. Draw round a penny in the middle of each circle and ask the children to colour this middle circle with a yellow crayon. Show them how to colour a thin 'rim' round the outer edge of the whole circle with a pink crayon. Fold the circle in half and then half again with the coloured side on the outside and help the children to cut thin vertical strips from the pink outer edge up to the edge of the yellow circle in the middle. Cut strips of the green activity paper (approx. 12cm × 1cm) for the stems. Give one stem to each child for them to write their first name on it, then use adhesive tape to attach the stem to the back of the daisy head in the centre. Make a vertical cut at the bottom end of each flower stem using the craft knife. Show the children how to thread their daisy at right angles into a friend's until all the daisies make a chain (as shown in the illustration). Flick some of the petals

upwards and inwards on each daisy before stapling the chain on to the background paper. Label the diagram 'Our daisy chain of friends'.

Discussion

A chain is a way of joining lots of separate pieces (usually metal) together and yet still allowing each piece or link to move. Can the children think of any uses for chains? (Bicycles, jewellery, hanging baskets.) How could the children make a chain of themselves? Show them how to link arms and let them sway from side to side as they sing a song together.

PATCHWORK CORNFIELDS

What you need

Blue background display paper on a display board, a stapler, a large sheet of flat cardboard, some corrugated cardboard, straw or hay (from a pet shop), rubber bands, adhesive and spreaders, scissors, scraps of fabric in different shades of green, grey and brown, and of different textures. The ribbing from corduroy material and the welts from odd socks or old woollen sweaters can be used to give the effect of furrows.

What to do

Cut the fabric strips and the corrugated card into irregular-shaped pieces to represent fields (maybe the children can do this). Let them arrange the pieces on the flat cardboard before actually sticking them on to it. The edges of the pieces should overlap to give the impression of separate fields in the landscape. Cut off any card edges which have not been covered by fabric and then staple the whole patchwork piece on to the blue background. Ask the children to take a handful of straw and fold it in half. Help them to secure this bundle with a rubber band and then to cut some straw off each end so that the bundle is roughly the cube shape of a bale of hay. Stick these bales of hay on to the foreground of the display.

Additions to the display

✧ Ask a child to draw a small tractor on brightly-coloured card, then cut it out and stick it onto one of the fields.

✧ Pull up some long grass, lay it flat and stick a strip of adhesive tape across the bottom. Turn it over and stick some adhesive tape on the other side. Stick this long grass 'sandwich' at the base of the cornfield picture.

✧ Cut some red tissue or crêpe paper into small irregular circles. The children can layer four circles on top of each other and secure them with a glass-headed pin through the centre. Crumple the petals to look like poppies. Pin these into the long grass.

✧ Add cotton wool clouds, a scarecrow and some wildlife.

A COLLAGE USING THINGS THAT GROW

What you need

A large piece of polystyrene left over from packing electronic equipment or domestic appliances (if it is a peculiar shape or has cut-outs this is fine), straw, old rubber gloves or balloons or very wide rubber bands, tissue and/or crêpe paper, a discarded woollen sweater or woollen socks, scraps of cotton fabric, some thick string, pencils, scissors.

What to do

Cut up the rubber gloves, woollen clothes, cotton scraps and paper into small squares (approx. 3cm × 3cm). Cut the string into 9cm lengths and let the children tie one knot in each piece. They can pull off little bunches of the straw as it is needed. Let the children push all these pieces randomly, and one at a time, into the polystyrene with the point of a pencil. The idea is to cover the top of the polystyrene as closely as possible with the squares. The result will be a collage of different colours and textures using only materials which have come from growing plants or animals. Different materials will need different pencil pressure and sometimes the point may go through the paper before it is pushed into the polystyrene. If this is likely to happen, fold the paper before pushing with the pencil. Hang the collage up with string.

Additions to the display

✧ If the polystyrene has a big enough cut-out section, write out the labels 'straw', 'rubber', 'paper', 'wool', 'cotton', 'string' on a piece of card and fix it into the hole. Alternatively, fit a map of the world into the space and run string from the materials to the countries where they are grown on the world map.

✧ Instead of mixing up the different materials on the polystyrene, keep each type together in a particular section.

✧ Stencil big alphabet letter shapes on to the polystyrene and ask the children to fill in these letters only.

BEAN SEQUENCE

What you need

A growing bean (see the activity on page 30), a piece of card to make a template of a glass jar (approx. 20cm × 89cm), six pieces of thick white paper (A4 size), pencil, felt-tipped pens, brown paper (an envelope will do) and green activity paper, scissors, six paper towels, adhesive and a spreader, a black marker pen, a ruler, a stapler, background paper fixed to the display area.

What to do

Make a cardboard template in the shape of a glass jar which the children can use each time they record the growth of the bean. The first picture in the sequence should be the bean on its own 'planted' in the jar. Position the template low down on a sheet of A4 paper and ask a child to pencil round the template and then to draw the same shape on to a paper towel. Another child can cut this jar shape out of the towel and stick it on to the paper jar outline. Cut out a brown paper 'bean' and stick it on to the paper towel. The second picture in the sequence will be the same as the first but the bean will have a sprouting root outline drawn with felt-tipped pen on to the paper towel. The third picture will have the addition of a growing shoot coloured in green. The fourth picture will show the shoot as a green coloured stem growing out of the jar and on to the paper above. (Remember that the root outline will also have grown longer and will have additional root hairs.) For the fifth picture, a child can cut out two green paper leaves and stick them on to the stalk above the neck of the jar. The sixth (the last) picture will have additional leaves and more root hairs.

Collect and save these pictures, which should be drawn as the children see a bean growing. Draw a black border as a frame for each picture, which the children can then arrange in a growing sequence. Write large clear numbers on each drawing and staple them in order on to the background paper.

Follow-up work

Ask questions about this picture sequence to help the children with direction, left and right, space words, size and comparison. Questions might include: What is happening in the picture to the left of number 3? Which picture comes after/before number 5? What is on the first picture? Which picture has the tallest bean/the least leaves/the biggest leaves/the longest root?

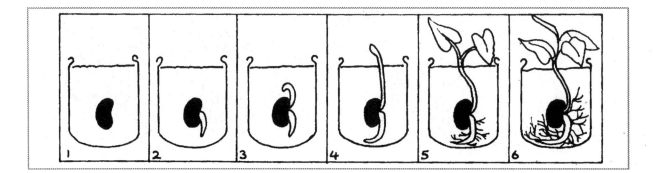

CHAPTER 8
ASSEMBLIES

Living things, including people, depend on each other for survival. Children cannot grow into healthy adults unless they socialise and interact with others. These assembly times can bring the children together to share what they have discovered about people, plants and animals growing.

PLANT GROWTH

The focus for this session is on growing in the natural world.

This assembly involves the children in drawing on experiences they may have already had during other activities, particularly practical tasks such as planting cress and mustard seeds or working with sequencing cards which depict the life cycle of a bean seed. These activities should have heightened their awareness of the wide variety of plants which grow in their immediate environment and beyond, helping them to reflect upon the fascinating developments at each stage of the growth cycle.

The assembly will work in a range of settings, and is suitable for a large gathering or a smaller group; if the weather is suitable, it could even take place outside in an environmental area or garden!

Introduction

The person leading the assembly should begin by helping the children to focus on the work they have already done on growing – perhaps by asking some of them to show the seeds they have germinated, display the pictures of butterflies they have made or show their models of the 'Three Little Pigs' houses.

If the assembly is taking place outside, the leader can also invite the children to point out the things around them which are growing.

What to do

Children dressed in appropriate colours, costumes or masks can depict the growth pattern of a plant through movement and/or dance. Tell them to curl up on the floor or ground and then gradually

rise up to represent the development of a seed or bulb into a fully-grown plant. Other children can take the roles of the rain and the sun in order to emphasise the importance of weather conditions in the growing process.

This movement work can be enhanced by simple background music — either pre-recorded or composed by the children themselves — and/or a commentary by the assembly leader.

Reflection

Invite the children to reflect on all the plants around them, whether they are real or representational, and consider what they need to make them grow successfully. Colour slides or OHPs could be shown in sequence to reveal the different stages in the life of a plant, or video footage of a flower emerging and opening could be played.

The reflection will be enhanced by a musical accompaniment which begins quietly and grows in texture and volume.

Prayer

It may be appropriate to invite some children to share in a prayer about the wonders of nature, in which they have an opportunity to thank God for the plants which grow and the sun and rain that they need. This could be structured to include the thoughts and prayers of the children themselves.

Songs

Most people who work with young children will already know a large number of songs about flowers and plants. It may be appropriate to select one which has links with the current season of the year. *Harlequin: 44 Songs Around The Year* (A & C Black) contains several songs which could be useful.

GETTING OLDER

The focus for this approach is on the ways in which children grow and develop in their early years.

The children will be drawing on their awareness of the ways in which they have changed in recent months and years and will also be encouraged to reflect on the ways in which those around them have grown bigger and taller.

Introduction

The person leading the assembly should invite the children to think back to when they were babies and toddlers and to consider how they have changed since those times — they have learned to walk and talk, they have grown taller, they need bigger clothes and shoes.

In a small group setting, it will be possible to invite a spontaneous response from the children, but with a larger gathering it may be more suitable to have done some preparation with the children in advance. Their ideas could then be expressed in a range of forms, such as mime or role-play, photograph collages of their lives, or through pictures and drawings.

What to do

The purpose of this activity is to give children an insight into the ways in which they grow and change, and to help them begin to understand some of the key elements of the life cycle of humans and other animals.

The leader reads or tells the story of *You'll soon grow into them, Titch* by Pat Hutchins (Puffin). If it is possible, some children could act out the roles of characters in the story, using appropriate props to enhance its meaning.

Titch has an older brother and sister; as they grow bigger, he inherits their cast-off clothes

which are still too large for him. He is delighted when his father buys him some clothes of his own which fit him perfectly; it is then Titch's turn to give his old clothes to his new baby brother who will also need to grow before they will fit him.

The leader should allow small groups of children time to examine and respond to the pictures which accompany the story as these focus on growth in other ways — mum's pregnancy gradually advances, she is growing more tired, a plant gets larger and a bird in a nest beyond the window raises her own family.

Reflection

The leader should encourage the children to think about how they have grown, linking their reflections with the experiences of Titch in the story. It may also be appropriate to refer to work done at other times on these same themes.

Prayer

Some children may wish to thank God for the ways in which they have grown and developed in their lives. The prayer could be based on the thoughts of the children themselves and read out by the person leading the gathering.

Songs

For those who require a song which is explicitly religious, 'He made me' from *Come and Praise* (BBC Publications) might be suitable. This song should be sung by those children who wish to profess their belief that they were made by God.

WHEN I GROW UP . . .

The focus for this approach is on growing up.

The assembly involves the children in thinking about the future and helps to prepare them for consideration of growth in the spiritual or personal spheres as well as the physical one.

The assembly will work in a range of settings, and with a fairly large gathering or with a smaller group.

Introduction

The person leading the assembly should invite the children to think about their lives; they should be encouraged to reflect on the way in which others — usually adults — take responsibility for them at every turn.

Children could suggest ways in which their families look after them — providing food and clothing, taking them to school or to the swimming baths, giving them pocket money.... They could express their ideas verbally or through pictures or short role-plays.

What to do

Individual children should be asked to come forward and share with the audience their thoughts about what they would like to do when they grow up. These might include their career ambitions, but could also feature their desires to be more independent – perhaps by choosing their own bedtimes, choosing what they want to eat or deciding on their style and type of clothing.

In a small group, this information could be offered through a simple discussion, but in a larger gathering a more structured format might be necessary. Children could show pictorial representations of their ideas or perhaps act them out using costumes and simple props.

Reflection

The leader should encourage the children to think about all the ways in which adults at home, school or elsewhere take care of them, using examples suggested by the children earlier in the session.

The children should then be asked to consider what it might be like to be grown-up, concentrating not only on the freedoms, but also the responsibilities of adult life.

Prayer

Some children may want to thank God for the way in which others love and care for them and also ask for blessings on their future lives as grown-ups. The leader should invite the children to offer their own prayers, or could write one for them using their suggestions.

Collective Worship in Schools

The assemblies outlined here are suitable for use with children in nurseries and playgroups, but would need to be adapted for use with pupils registered in schools. As a result of legislation enacted in 1944, 1988 and 1993, there are now specific points, to be observed when developing a programme of Collective Acts of Worship in a school.

Further guidance will be available from your local SACRE – Standing Advisory Council for RE.

ACTION RHYMES AND POEMS

GROWING FLOWERS

First we dig the soil,
Then we plant the seeds,
We water them regularly,
And pull up the weeds.

Soon some tiny shoots,
Push out of the ground,
Reaching for the sun,
Growing without a sound.

At last the buds appear,
Closed up all tight,
Slowly they open up,
Into a wonderful sight.

Karen King

Actions
The children stand in a line and do the following actions.
Verse 1: The children pretend to dig the soil, then plant the seeds, water the garden, pull up some weeds.
Verse 2: The children bend their knees and crouch down, then start standing up slowly, and stretch their arms in the air.
Verse 3: The children half-cover their faces with their hands then slowly move their hands away from their faces and stretch their arms out wide, smiling.

PHOTOCOPIABLE RESOURCES

GARDEN RAINBOW

There's a rainbow in my garden
Flowers of every hue
The pinks are pink, the roses are red
The violets are blue

Here are some orange marigolds
The shoots and leaves are green
And look — a tiny purple flower
The smallest one I've seen

By the hedge the buttercups
Are shining gold and bright
The daisies peeking through the grass
Are showing petals white

Look at all the colours
Glowing in the sun
Growing in the garden
Until the day is done

And when the sun has gone to bed
The flowers are tired too
They close their petals, droop their heads
And go to sleep like you.

Fiona McGarry

Actions
Verse 1: The children sweep an arm in an arc to make a rainbow.
Verse 2: The children form fingers into the shape of tiny shoots/flowers growing. On 'look' they shade their eyes with one hand and point as if discovering a hidden flower.
Verse 3: On 'peeking' the children put fingers round eyes as if looking through glasses or binoculars.
Verse 4: The children shade their eyes with a hand again and look around, then extend their arms upwards as if growing.
Verse 5: The children wrap their arms around their head, droop their head and pretend to go to sleep.

DAISY CHAIN

Ten dancing daisies
Growing in a line
The wind blew one of them away
Then there were nine

Nine dancing daisies
By the garden gate
A hungry goat had one for lunch
Then there were eight

Eight dancing daisies
When along came Kevin
He took one home for his mum
Then there were seven

Seven dancing daisies
One got in a fix
She fell down and broke her stem
Then there were six

Six dancing daisies
In front of the beehive
A busy bee buzzed into one
Then there were five

Five dancing daisies
When the rain began to pour
One was washed out in the storm
Then there were four

Four dancing daisies
Happy as can be
A butterfly sat down on one
Then there were three

Three dancing daisies
Wondering what to do
I put one behind my ear
Then there were two

Two dancing daisies
Swaying in the sun
A bird used one to line her nest
Then there was one

One dancing daisy
Standing all alone
She went to join a daisy chain
Then there were none!

Fiona McGarry

Actions

Choose ten children to stand in the centre of the ring as the 'daisies'. Point to each daisy in turn to leave the daisy chain and return to join the rest of the group.

Verse 1: Blow one of the daisies away.
Verse 2: Munch as if eating a daisy.
Verse 3: Stoop as if to pick a flower.
Verse 4: Bend suddenly from the waist.
Verse 5: With forefinger and thumb together, imitate the flight of a bee landing on a flower.
Verse 6: Use hands and fingers to imitate rain falling.
Verse 7: Pretend to be a butterfly. Sit down.
Verse 8: Place one finger on chin as if 'wondering', then pretend to put a flower behind their ear.
Verse 9: Flap arms like birds' wings.
Verse 10: All join hands to make one long chain.

WHEN I WAS A BABY

When I was a baby
I was small, small, small
Now that I am bigger
I am tall, tall, tall
I'm not as tall as Mummy, or Daddy, or a
tree
I'm really just the right size for me!

When I was a baby
I would sleep all day
Now that I am bigger
All I want to do is play
No cooking and no cleaning and no driving
the car
I like things just the way they are!

Jan Jones

> **Actions**
> Children mime stretching, curling actions, and so
> on, as suggested in the poem.

THE CROP SONG

This is the song
the seed sings:
SOW, SOW, SOW.
(Sow seeds from a basket.)

This is the song
the shoot sings:
grow, grow, grow.
*(Slowly raise a hand upwards, with twisty arm
movement.)*

This is the song
the root sings:
deep, deep, deep.
*(Point hand downwards and lower arm slowly, to
mimic root.)*

And this is the song
the farmer sings:
reap, reap, reap.
(Gather sheaves into arms, or drive tractor.)

Tony Mitton

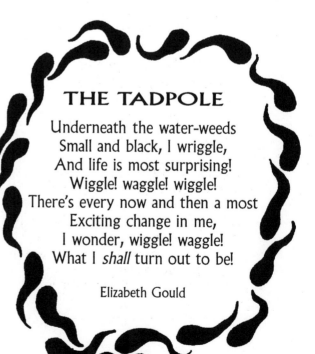

THE TADPOLE

Underneath the water-weeds
Small and black, I wriggle,
And life is most surprising!
Wiggle! waggle! wiggle!
There's every now and then a most
Exciting change in me,
I wonder, wiggle! waggle!
What I *shall* turn out to be!

Elizabeth Gould

A SEEDY STORY

In the dark, dark earth
was a small, small seed.
And the sun came up
and the rain came down.

From the small, small seed
burst a white, white root.
And the sun came up
and the root pushed down.

From the small, small seed
crept a brave, brave shoot.
And the shoot grew up
and the rain came down.

From the damp, damp soil
crept the brave, brave shoot.
And the shoot grew green
and the sun shone down.

From the green, green shoot
grew a tall, tall tree.
And the sun came up
and the rain came down.

On the tall, tall tree
grew A PLUM for me!
And the sun came up
and the sun came down.

Judith Nicholls

BIRTHDAYS

Every year another candle
added to your birthday cake.
How old are you now, I wonder?
How many birthdays does that make?

Getting bigger, growing taller,
larger shoes to fit your feet,
every year we all grow older,
birthdays are a special treat.

Fun and games and happy faces
lots of presents from our friends,
every year we all have birthdays,
let's hope birthdays never end.

Jan Pollard

Actions
The children can act out this poem in pairs. Child 1
is the seed, starting curled up and using one hand for
the root, the other for the shoot, gradually stretching
higher and stretching arms out. One hand can be
used to make a plum shape. Child 2 (or an adult) is
the sun and rain, using arms and hands for appropriate
actions — then picking the plum at the end!

The poem can be arranged as two-line verses if
preferred.

GROWN OUT OF

My trousers are too tight,
they just won't fit.

And my jumper?
I've grown out of it.

My shirt's too short,
it just won't do.

There are holes in my socks
where my toes push through.

It's lucky I don't grow out of my skin.
'Cos then there'd be *nothing*
to put me in!

Tony Mitton

THE FARMER KNOWS

The farmer loves
the falling rain.
He knows it helps
to grow the grain.

The farmer loves
the shining sun.
It feeds his growing plants,
each one.

The farmer loves
the rich, brown earth.
He knows what soil
is really worth.

With these good things,
the farmer knows,
everything lives,
everything grows.

Tony Mitton

THE PLANTER

With a truckful of trees
labelled 'Handle with Care',
I head for the hills
and the fine forest air.

With a spade in my hand
I dig out a hole
to cradle my oak
in the fine forest soil.

With fingers and thumbs
I loosen the roots,
then gently press down
with fine forest boots.

My feet are in bluebells,
my head's in the sky;
my arms full of seedlings —
this forest won't die!

Judith Nicholls

ONE DAY (WHEN I GROW UP)

One day
when I grow up
I'll take a trip.

I'll hop on a bus
(no fuss)
then take a ship.

The ship will sail me
far away ...
but not just now,
no, not today.

For now,
I think I'll stay.

But one day
when I grow up
I'll travel far.

I'll jump in a car and say, 'Ta-ta',
then take a train
or p'raps a plane.

The plane will fly me
through the air
and then I'll end up,
well ... *somewhere.*

Yes, one day
when I grow up
I'll travel round the world.
That's the life for me.

But just for now
I think I'll stay at home
because I'm only three.

Besides,
it's nearly time for tea.

Tony Mitton

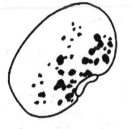

THE BEAN SEED

The bean seed
Is black and purple
Like a bruise.

It lies in the palm of my hand
Like a tiny rugby ball,
Its skin as smooth
As an egg-shell.

Last month,
I planted one in a pot,
Patting the soil
Firmly around it.
I have watered it regularly,
Watching and waiting,
Wondering if anything has been going on
Down there under the soil.

Has the seed really split open?
Has it really put down roots?
Is it really growing a shoot?

Yesterday, when I looked,
There was a tiny blade of green
Pushing through the soil.
Now I know
That one day
My bean seed will grow
Into a tall beanstalk
That will produce red flowers
And bean seeds of its own.

John Foster

THE BALLOON

Hold the neck gently,
Blow! Blow! Blow!
Watch the balloon
Grow, grow, grow.

Pinch the neck tightly,
Tie it with string
To keep all the air
In, in, in.

Hold the string tightly,
Don't let it go!
Or away, away, away
Your balloon will blow!

John Foster

STORIES

ALEXANDER'S GROWING-UP DAY

He was the smallest person in the family. Everyone called him Sprout.

'Come on Sprout, get in the car,' Mother would call. 'We've got to take the girls to school.'

'Gee up, Sprout,' Father would shout. 'It's time to fetch the girls from swimming.'

'Chop, chop, Sprout,' Grandpa would cry. 'We must hurry to the post office before it shuts.'

'Get a move on Sprout,' Jessica would yell. 'Hannah and I are going to our ballet class.'

'What are you doing now, Sprout?' Hannah would shriek. 'You are going to make us all LATE!'

To Sprout the whole world seemed to be in a hurry. He never had time to finish anything.

One day, when Sprout was three, Mother took him to nursery school.

'This is Alexander,' she said to the teacher.

Sprout looked all about him. But there was no-one else there.

'Goodbye. Be a good boy,' said Mother as she kissed him and rushed off.

The teacher took his hand. 'Come along, Alexander,' she said. 'Come and meet the other children.'

Alexander walked with her along the hall and through a doorway.

'This is Alexander,' she said.

'Hello Alexander,' cried the children.

Sprout looked at the teacher.

'I think you have a lovely name,' said the teacher.

Sprout smiled. 'I'm Alexander!' he said.

'Would you like a seat, Alexander?' asked the teacher. 'We have lots of puzzles and lovely fat crayons too.'

Alexander spent a long time drawing a picture. He drew dragons and stars and a hairy monster. When he had quite finished that he did a puzzle. He took a long time to work it out but no-one told him to hurry up.

He stood with the children to choose a drink. Then they all went out to play. In the playground there were bicycles to ride and trucks to push and pull and a big red slide. Alexander had such fun.

When play time was over they all sat on the floor.

'It's group time now,' said the teacher, 'and I'm going to read you a story.'

'Good!' shouted the children. Alexander smiled. He loved stories.

At half past twelve his Grandpa came to fetch him. 'Had a good morning then, Sprout?' he asked.

Alexander said nothing.

'Cat got your tongue, Sprout?' asked Grandpa.

'Sprout,' said Alexander, 'has gone away. I'm grown into Alexander.'

'I see,' said Grandpa.

After lunch Grandpa got a long piece of paper. On it in big letters he wrote ALEXANDER'S ROOM.

'There you are,' he said. 'We'll pin it on your door. Then everyone will know.'

'Thanks Grandpa,' said Alexander. 'We could make one for your door too. What's your name?'

'George Henry Archibald Montgomery,' said Grandpa.

'I don't think we've got a long enough piece of paper for all that,' said Alexander, 'and I'm a bit tired.'

'How about 40 winks?' asked Grandpa.

Alexander nodded. He got his blanket and his teddy. He lay on the sofa and closed his eyes.

At tea-time everyone came rushing in.

'Hullo Sprout!' yelled Hannah.

'Had a good time, Sprout?' shouted Jessica.

'What did you do at nursery, Sprout, darling?' asked Mother.

'If you'll all be very quiet,' said Grandpa, 'Alexander will tell you all about it.'

'WHO?' asked the girls.

'ME!' said Alexander. 'I'm grown much bigger now and my proper name is on my door.'

He smiled at them all.

'And Alexander has had a wonderful, special day,' he said.

Ruth Silvestre

PHOTOCOPIABLE RESOURCES

THE ENORMOUS TURNIP

Once upon a time there was an old man who planted a turnip seed in the ground and waited for it to grow.

First it grew into a small turnip, then a middling turnip, then a big turnip, then a bigger turnip and then an enormous turnip! The old man decided that it was time to pull the turnip up and eat it.

So he took hold of the turnip and pulled. But the turnip stayed in the ground.

The old man took a better grip and pulled harder. The turnip stayed in the ground.

Then the old man gritted his teeth and pulled and pulled and pulled, until he had no pull left in him. But the turnip stayed in the ground.

So the old man went to his wife and said, 'Wife, come and help me pull up this turnip.'

So the old woman went with him back to the turnip. She took hold of the old man, the old man took hold of the turnip and they pulled. They pulled again.

They pulled and they pulled and they pulled, until they had no pull left in them. And the turnip stayed in the ground.

So the old woman went and found her granddaughter and said, 'Granddaughter, come and help us pull up this turnip.'

The granddaughter went back with the old woman. She took hold of the old woman, the old woman took hold of the old man, the old man took hold of the turnip, and they got ready. 'Now let's try tugging,' said the old man.

So they tugged.

They TUGGED and they TUGGED and they TUGGED, until none of them had any tug left. And the turnip stayed in the ground.

So the granddaughter went and found the dog. 'Dog,' she said, 'come and help us tug this turnip up.' The dog went with the girl back to the turnip.

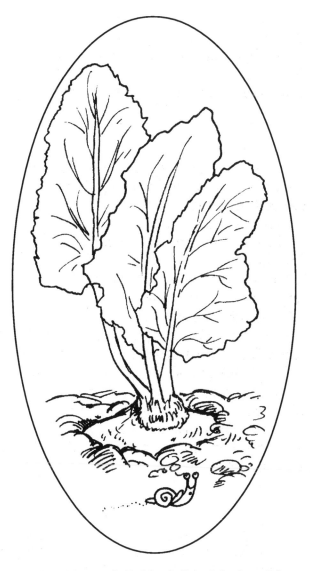

The dog took hold of the girl, the girl took hold of the old woman, the old woman took hold of the old man, the old man took hold of the turnip, and they all got ready. 'Let's try heaving,' said the old man.

So they heaved at the turnip.

They HEAVED, and they HEAVED, and they HEAVED.

HEAVE ...

HEAVE ...

HEAVE ... until none of them had any heave left in them. And the turnip stayed in the ground.

So the dog went away and found the cat and said, 'Cat, come and help us heave at this turnip.' The cat went with the dog back to the turnip.

PHOTOCOPIABLE RESOURCES

The cat took hold of the dog, the dog took hold of the girl, the girl took hold of the old woman, the old woman took hold of the old man, the old man took hold of the turnip, and they all got ready. 'Let's try dragging it this time.'

So they dragged at the turnip.

They dragged again.

And the turnip came up out of the ground!

And the cat fell on the ground, the dog fell on the cat, the girl fell on the dog, the old woman fell on her granddaughter and the old man fell on his wife, and the turnip fell on the old man.

It took all of them to pull, tug, heave and drag the turnip into the house. There they cut it up and made it into turnip soup. There was more than enough for everyone, and for all I know, the old man, the old woman, their granddaughter, the dog and the cat have lived on turnip soup from that day to this, and are all eating huge bowlfuls of turnip soup this very minute, even as you are listening to this story.

But that's enough of turnips, and the end of the story.

Retold by Susan Price — from the *Kingfisher Treasury of Nursery Stories*

GROW UP!

'Why don't you grow up!'

Tim stood in the puddle of water in the very clean kitchen. He looked at his Mum's face. She was red and hot and her hair was standing up in tufts.

Tim went away. It wasn't his fault. He had been helping. The bowl of water slipped. It wasn't *his* fault.

Tim sat in his secret place in the shed and thought.

'How do you grow up?' he asked. He shrugged his shoulders and sighed.

Out in the garden he stopped by the flowers. Crouching down he said, 'How did you grow up?'

They waved to him and whispered. He leaned close but it was a secret. They wouldn't tell him. He shrugged his shoulders and sighed.

Next he went into the greenhouse. The curled-up cat purred.

'How did you grow up?'

'Purr,' the cat answered. Tim didn't speak cat words. He stroked the soft fur then he shrugged his shoulders and sighed.

Next he went to Dad, sitting at the computer.

'Dad, how did you grow up?'

'What? Tim, I'm working. Ask your mother.'

Tim stood and looked at his father then he shrugged his shoulders and sighed.

Finally, he went to Gramps. Gramps was sitting in his big armchair in his room. He was reading the newspaper. Tim shrugged his shoulders and sighed. He turned to walk out.

'Tim?' Gramps asked. 'What is it?'

'I wanted to ask you something. And it is important.'

'Ask me then.'

'How did you grow up?'

'Bit by bit,' Gramps said. 'It took a long time.'

Tim climbed on Gramps' lap and wriggled to get comfortable.

He told Gramps all about it, how he had made Mum cross and she had told him to grow up. How he had asked the flowers but they wouldn't tell. How he had asked the cat and he had told him, but in cat words. And how he had asked Dad but he was too busy.

Tim stopped talking and looked up into Gramps' crinkled face. Putting up his small hand he stroked Gramps' rough, scratchy chest.

'It's been ages since Mum told me to grow up and I haven't grown up at all.'

'Yes, you have,' Gramps told him. 'Get down. I've something to show you.'

Tim scrambled down and helped his grandad as he heaved himself slowly out of his chair. Hand in hand they went to the big wooden chest of drawers. There Gramps showed him a picture. It was a baby lying in Gramps' arms.

Tim looked up at Gramps then shrugged his shoulders and sighed. It was just a picture of a baby.

'That's you, Tim. When you were a baby.'

Tim looked at the picture. He let go of Gramps' hand and went to the mirror. Then he went back to Gramps.

'I'm not like that anymore.'

'No, Tim. You've grown up.'

'I've grown up?' Tim cried.

'Yes, and you will grow up some more until you are as tall as Daddy.'

Tim smiled. He didn't shrug his shoulders, he didn't sigh, but he did hug his Gramps.

Gillian Goddard

PETRA'S ROOM

Petra had a lovely bedroom. It was small and cosy and it was full of all the things that Petra loved best.

'A bit too full,' laughed Mum, but Petra wouldn't let her take anything out of it.

She wouldn't let her take away the quilt she'd had when she was a baby. She wouldn't let her take away the mobiles hanging from her ceiling. She wouldn't let her take away the cuddly toys that were tucked down the side of her bed and piled up against the end wall. She wouldn't let her take away anything.

One day at school, her friend Jonathan told her that he was changing bedrooms soon.

Petra was horrified. 'Why?' she asked.

'Because my bedroom is TITCHY,' said Jonathan. 'And I'm getting bigger, so I need a bigger bedroom. I'm going to have a new carpet and new curtains and new wallpaper and a new lampshade and —'

Petra burst into tears. It sounded horrible!

In the night, she had bad dreams and shouted so loudly that Mum came running into her room.

'I don't want to grow up,' she cried, as Mum wrapped the duvet round them both to keep warm. 'I don't want to get bigger. I don't want to move out of my lovely bedroom.'

'Then you shan't,' soothed Mum. 'Not if you don't want to.'

Soon it was Petra's birthday and she had lots of presents. There were new toys, new games and new clothes. Petra had a bit of trouble fitting them all into her room.

When Petra went to play with Jonathan, he showed her his new bedroom.

Petra looked around it carefully. 'It's just like your old room,' she said in surprise. 'But it's bigger.'

At home, Mum had some news.

'Guess what!' she said. 'We're going to have a new baby a couple of months after Christmas.'

Petra was very pleased. She'd wanted a baby brother or sister for a long time.

For Christmas, Petra got more toys and more games and more clothes. Her little bedroom was bursting!

'Mum,' she said. 'If I change bedrooms, which bed will I sleep in?'

'Your own, of course,' said Mum. 'We'll move it with you. And we'll move your cupboard and drawers, and probably get some extra matching ones if the new bedroom is big enough.'

'And will I keep my own pictures?' asked Petra.

'Of course you will!' laughed Mum. 'Your own pictures, your own mobiles, your own toys and your own lampshade.'

'And if I don't like it, can I move back?' asked Petra.

'Of course you can,' said Mum.

So at the weekend they moved every single thing out of Petra's little room into her bigger one. Petra lay down on the bed.

'Mum,' she said, excitedly. 'It looks just like my other room — but bigger!'

Petra found that there was lots of spare space on the walls for new pictures, and there was room for two more cupboards to put her clothes and games and toys in.

'There's only one problem now,' said Mum. 'Where will we put the baby when it's born?'

'In my old room, of course,' said Petra. 'Shall I draw it some pictures?'

'That's a lovely idea,' said Mum.

Jan Jones

SONGS

A BRAND NEW BABY

There's a brand new ba-by _____ in my mum-my, _____ She says she felt a flut-ter-ing in her tum-my, _____ She says it is grow-ing night and day _____ and then _____ in the Spring it will come out to play.

Lesley Funge

COUNT THE RINGS

Quite quick

Do you know just how old the trees are? Are they ve-ry old or are they ve-ry new?

Do you know just how old the trees are? Here's a lit-tle sec-ret, this is what you do.

Count the rings. Round and round they go. Ev-'ry year means an-oth-er ring will grow.

Count the rings. Round and round they go. Count the rings then you ought to know.

Clive Barnwell

PHOTOCOPIABLE RESOURCES

GRANDAD LOVES HIS GARDEN

Brightly

1. Grand - dad loves his gar - den, you will find him ev - 'ry day,
Work - ing hard out in the yard and whist - l - ing a - way.

Chorus

Dig - ging and ra - king,___ siev - ing and sha - king,___ plant - ing the seeds___ in a row,
Wat - er - ing weed - ing and spray - ing and feed - ing and watch - ing the gar - den grow.

2. Grandad says it keeps him fit
And out of mischief too
Whatever kind of weather
There are always things to do.

Chorus
Digging and raking ....

Debbie Campbell

SAVINGS GROW!

Unaccompanied

One pence in! Two pence in! Hold your coins___ by the slot and drop them in!
Sav - ings grow in - side your mon - ey box or tin, Hold your coins___ by the slot and drop them in!

Words – Sue Nicholls
Tune – Hot Cross Buns

PHOTOCOPIABLE RESOURCES

CLOMP! STOMP! TROMPERTY TROMP!

Clive Barnwell

2. I am a great big dinosaur
From ever so long ago.
I break the trees and crush the plants
That lie on the ground below.
I paddle in the rivers
And I go where I want to go.
I am a great big dinosaur
From ever so long ago.

Chorus

DINGLE, DANGLE SCARECROW

Not too fast

He's a din - gle, dan - gle scare - crow, with a din - gle, dan - gle head

With his din - gle, dan - gle shoul - ders, and his din - gle, dan - gle legs.

He's got din - gle, dan - gle fin - gers on his din - gle, dan - gle hands

And all day long in the din - gle, dan - gle fields Din - gle, Dan - gle Scare - crow stands.

Clive Barnwell

DANDELION CLOCK

Dan - de - lion clock, dan - de - lion clock, wait - ing for the wind to blow.

Dan - de - lion clock, dan - de - lion clock, now your seeds are read - y to go.

Ev - ery lit - tle seed has a pa - ra - chute. It flies a - way through the air. If it

falls in the *gar - den and makes a root, there'll be an - oth - er plant next year to make a

For further verses discuss places where the dandelion might take root (and where it wouldn't).
Replace the word garden with other places, e.g. 'field' or 'park'.

Jan Holdstock

GROWING UP

When we were ba-bies we were ve-ry ve-ry small. We just waved our lit-tle hands and said 'Goo goo'.

Now we are ** years old we're grow-ing ve-ry tall, And we'll show you all the things that we can do.

We can clap our hands.

We can stamp our feet.

Jan Holdstock

At ** sing the children's age.
If some of the children are older than others, sing a different age in each verse.

At * insert two different actions in each verse.
The verses can be cumulative if you like.

If you are talking about babies, you may like to replace 'waved our little hands' with other suitable actions.

THE SUNFLOWER SONG

Unhurriedly

1. Got - ta sun - flow'r seed in my hand. Got - ta sun - flow'r seed in my hand. Got - ta sun - flow'r seed, got - ta sun - flow'r seed, got - ta sun - flow'r seed in my hand.

2. Gotta sunflow'r seed in the ground.
3. Gotta sunflow'r shoot in the air.
4. Gotta sunflow'r head in the sky.
5. Gotta sunflow'r in my hand.

Sue Nicholls

THE THREE LITTLE PIGS

Pig: 1. I've heard a - bout that big bad wolf but I'm not a - fraid. I got my - self a pile of straw and look at the house, look at the house, look at the house I made. *Wolf:* The lit - tle pig made his house of straw but that's not strong e - nough. I think that I can blow it down, I'll huff and puff.

Jan Holdstock

A SEED

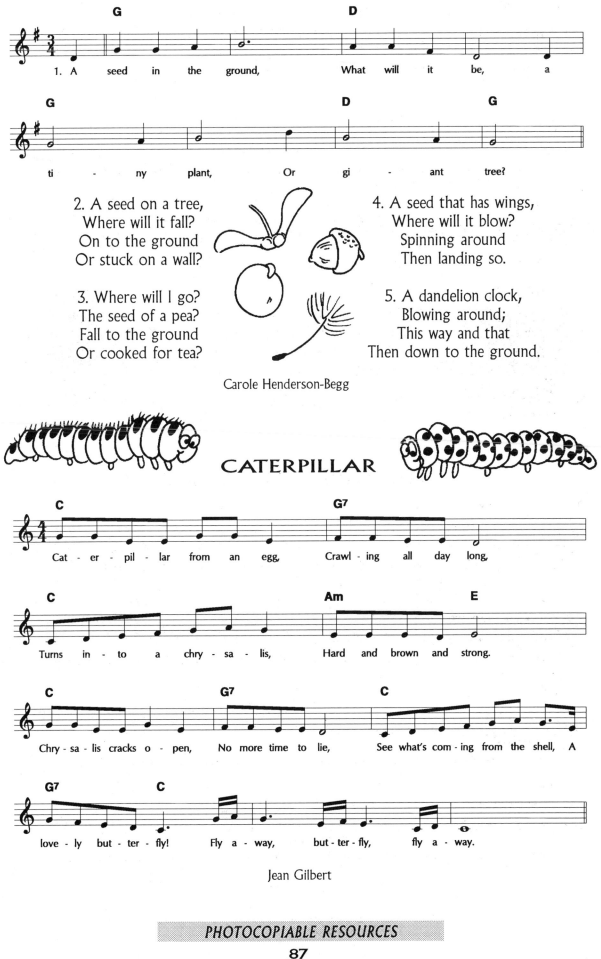

1. A seed in the ground, What will it be, a ti - ny plant, Or gi - ant tree?

2. A seed on a tree,
   Where will it fall?
   On to the ground
   Or stuck on a wall?

3. Where will I go?
   The seed of a pea?
   Fall to the ground
   Or cooked for tea?

4. A seed that has wings,
   Where will it blow?
   Spinning around
   Then landing so.

5. A dandelion clock,
   Blowing around;
   This way and that
   Then down to the ground.

Carole Henderson-Begg

CATERPILLAR

Cat - er - pil - lar from an egg, Crawl - ing all day long,

Turns in - to a chry - sa - lis, Hard and brown and strong.

Chry - sa - lis cracks o - pen, No more time to lie, See what's com - ing from the shell, A

love - ly but - ter - fly! Fly a - way, but - ter - fly, fly a - way.

Jean Gilbert

PHOTOCOPIABLE RESOURCES

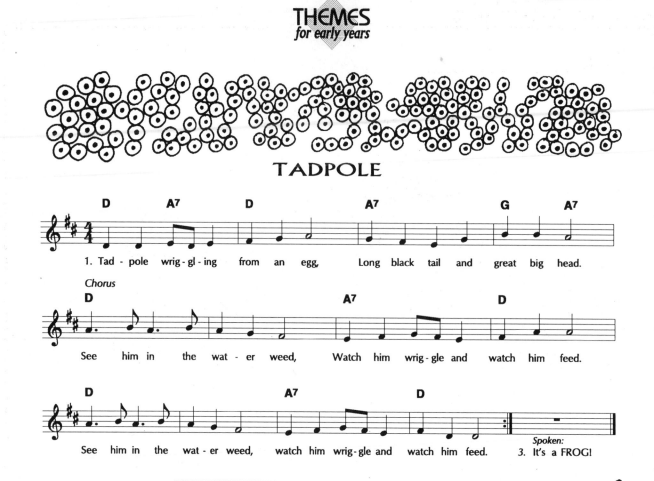

TADPOLE

1. Tad - pole wrig - gl - ing from an egg, Long black tail and great big head.

Chorus

See him in the wat - er weed, Watch him wrig - gle and watch him feed.

See him in the wat - er weed, watch him wrig-gle and watch him feed. *Spoken:* 3. It's a FROG!

2. Shrinking tail and growing limbs,
Tadpole's changing as he swims.
See him in the water-weed,
Watch him wriggle and watch him feed.
See him in the water-weed,
Watch him wriggle and watch him feed.

3. Lost his tail but now he's found,
Strong back legs to jump around.
Jumping high into a bush,
Jumping into the water, splash!
Jumping high into a bush,
Jumping into the water, splash!
It's a FROG! (spoken)

Jean Gilbert

Growing up

THEMES
for early years

Name _____

Building a body

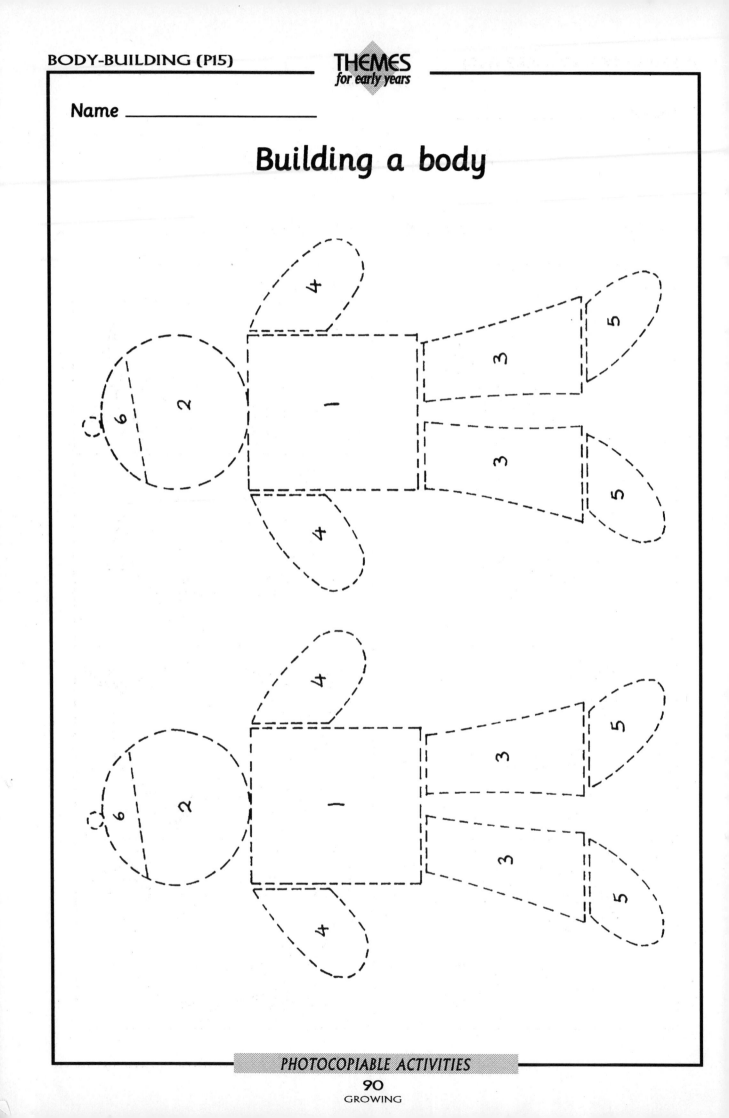

THEMES
for early years

Whose baby is it?

◆ Match the adult animal to the baby animal.

THEMES
for early years

Growing roots

✦ Draw in the roots as they branch out to find water.
Remember to go round the stones.

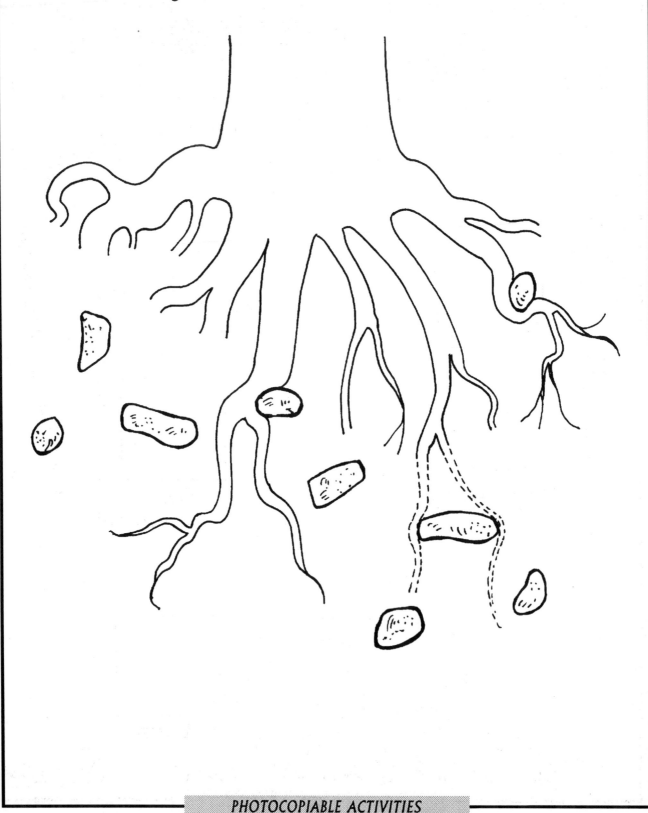

THEMES
for early years

Name _____

Our tree home

✦ Match the pictures to the names.

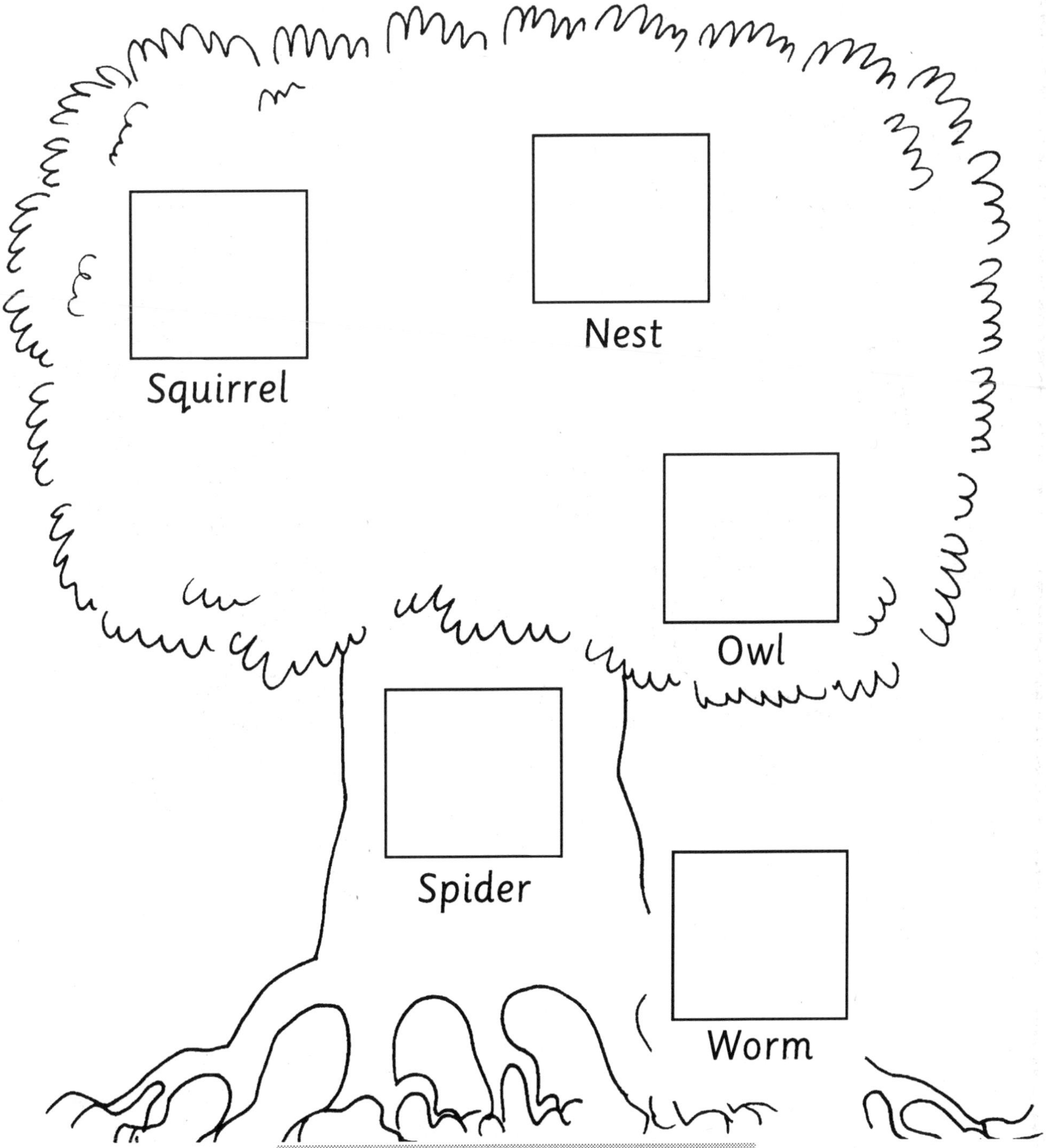

Squirrel

Nest

Owl

Spider

Worm

THEMES
for early years

Apple bingo

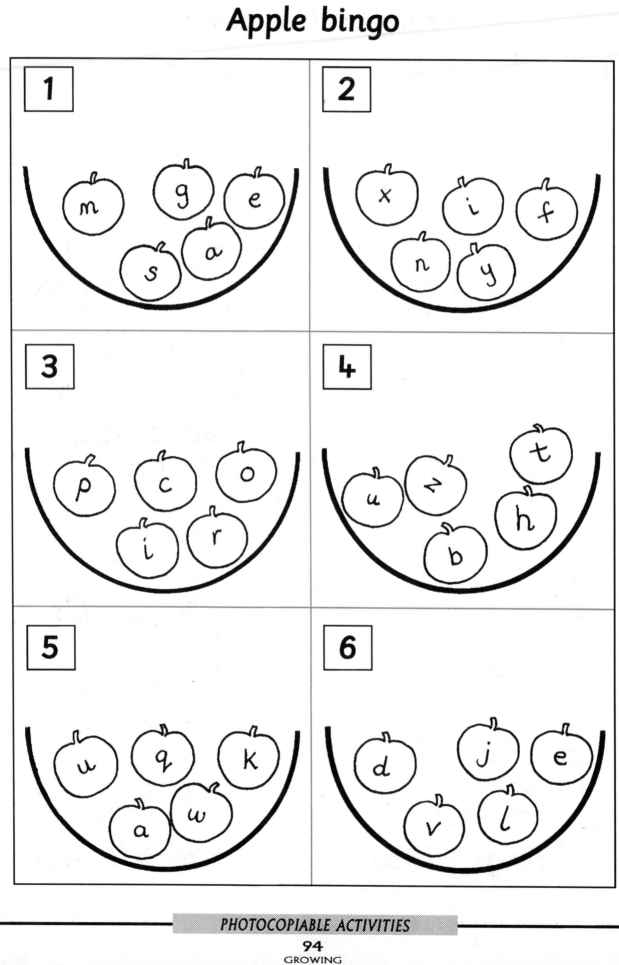

Name _____

Playing the game

✦ Draw lines to match the games equipment.

□ balls left over

□ shuttlecocks left over

□ rings left over

□ hoops left over

RECOMMENDED MATERIALS

POETRY

'The swing' from *A Child's Garden Of Verses*
R.L. Stevenson (Wordsworth).
Dinosaur Poems J. Foster and K. Paul (OUP).
'The morning walk', 'Forgiven', 'Wind on the hill'
and 'When I was one' from *Now We Are Six*
A.A. Milne (Methuen).
'A seed', 'Newspapers', 'Can you walk on tiptoe?'
and 'The flower seller' from *Seeing and Doing
Anthology* 1977 Thames Television (out of print).
'The dinosaur', 'Pussy willows', 'Mrs Brown' and
'The harvest' from *Seeing and Doing New
Anthology* 1982 Thames Television (out of print).
'Eggs for breakfast', 'The acorn', 'Apple
blossoms', 'Haytime', 'The shiny little house' and
'A sea song from the shore' from *The Book of a
Thousand Poems* (Collins).
'Tinker tailor' and 'If all the world was paper'
from *The Oxford Nursery Rhyme Book*
assembled by Iona and Peter Opie.
'House coming down', 'Extremely naughty
children' and 'When I grow up' from *The Young
Puffin Book of Verse* compiled by Barbara Ireson.
'Little Arabella Miller', 'I have a little spider', 'One
potato two potato', 'Old Tom Tomato', 'A hive
for a honey bee', 'Five fluffy chicks', 'Wind the
bobbin up' and 'Who's that tickling my back?' from
This Little Puffin compiled by Elizabeth Matterson.
'Growing up', 'The King's breakfast', 'Happiness'
and 'There's a wide eyed owl' from *When We
Were Very Young* A.A. Milne (Methuen).

MUSIC AND SONGS

'Bananas in pyjamas' from *Apusskidu: 56 Songs
For Children* (A&C Black).
'Under a web', 'Falling leaves' and 'Red Balloons'
from *Count Me In* (A&C Black).
'Butterfly butterfly', 'Five little freckled frogs',
'Turn the rope', 'When I was one' and 'One
elephant one fine day' from *Knock At The Door*
J. Betts (Ward Lock).
'Hokey cokey', 'Oats and beans and barley grow',
'In and out the dusty bluebells', 'The farmer's in
his den', 'The scarecrow' and 'The big ship sails
on the Alley Alley O' from *Oranges and
Lemons* compiled by K. King (OUP) and tape of
party games.
'The cherry tree', 'Five fat peas' and 'The apple
tree' from *Round and Round the Garden*
S. Williams (OUP) and tape of 40 play rhymes.

'Bobby Shafto' from *Sing Hey diddle diddle*
(A&C Black).
'At half past three we go home to tea' and
'Think of a world without any flowers' from
Someone's Singing Lord (A&C Black).
'Her we go gathering nuts in May' from
The Oxford Nursery Song Book (OUP).
'Frogs jump', 'The cabbage patch', 'The
supermarket', 'Each India rubber ball', 'Help me
wind my ball of wool', 'After a bath', 'Puff the
magic dragon' and 'Sowing beans' from *Up, up
and away* D. Pearson (OUP).

STORIES AND PICTURE BOOKS

Are You my Mother P.D. Eastman (HarperCollins).
Baby Goz S. Weatherill (Lincoln).
Farm Alphabet Book J. Miller (Dent).
Frog and Toad are Friends A. Lobel (Mammoth).
Funnybones J. & A. Ahlberg (Mammoth).
It's My Birthday H. Oxenbury (Walker).
Jack and the Beanstalk (Ladybird Favourite Tales).
Kingfisher Treasury of Nursery Stories S. Price.
Mrs Wobble the Waitress A. Ahlberg (Puffin).
One day with Mummy H. Oxenbury (Walker).
Tall Inside J. Richardson (Puffin).
The complete farmyard tales H. Amery and
S. Cartwright (Usborne).
The Tale of Mr Jeremy Fisher B. Potter (Puffin).
The Ugly Duckling (Ladybird Favourite Tales).
The Very Hungry Caterpillar E. Carle (Picture
Puffin).
Titch P. Hutchins (Picture Puffin).

INFORMATION AND IDEAS

Animals M. Gooday and M. Collin (PPA).
Children's Brittanica.
Copycat S. Kilroy (Picture Puffin).
Dinosaurs A. Royston (Dorling Kindersley).
Growing Food C. Llewellyn (Simon & Schuster).
Plants and how they grow (Ladybird).
Pond Life J. Coldrey (Collins).
Puppy J. Burton (Dorling Kindersley).
See the Daisies Feel the Rain E. Goddard (PPA).
Things that Grow M. Halson (Collins).
Trees L. Gamlin (Dorling Kindersley).
Trees G. Hall (Headway Hodder & Stoughton).
Vegetables created by P. de Bourgoing (Moonlight).
What makes a flower grow S. Mayes (Usborne
Starting Point Science).

PHOTOCOPIABLE RESOURCES